KU-779-626

ARNE & CARLOS

KNITTED
DOLLS

Northamptonshire
DISCARDED
Libraries

Northamptonshire
DISCARDED
Libraries

Search Press

8000321646

Northamptonshire
Libraries & Information
Services
NW

Askews & Holts

Contents

First published in Great Britain in 2012 by Search Press
Limited, Wellwood, North Farm Road, Tunbridge Wells,
Kent TN2 3DR

Also published in the United States of America in 2012 by
Trafalgar Square Books
North Pomfret, Vermont 05053

Originally published in Norwegian as Strikkedukker by
Cappelen Damm A/S

© 2011 Cappelen Damm A/S
English translation © 2012 Trafalgar Square Books

ISBN: 978-1-84448-850-6

All rights reserved. No part of this book, text, photographs
or illustrations may be reproduced, or transmitted in any
form or by any means by print, photoprint, internet or
in any other way known or as yet unknown, or stored in
a retrieval system, without written permission obtained
beforehand from Search Press.

The sources mentioned in this book refer to those
organisations that supplied the materials and equipment
used by the authors. Many of these organisations provide
on-line ordering facilities and distribute worldwide.
However, all of the materials and equipment used in this
book can be readily obtained from alternative sources,
including specialist stores, on-line suppliers and mail-
order companies.

Translation: Carol Huebscher Rhoades
Illustrations: Arne & Carlos
Photography: Ragnar Hartvig
Styling: Ingrid Skaansar
Book Design: Gina Rose Design

Printed in China

10 9 8 7 6 5 4 3 2 1

ONE OF SEVERAL SUITCASES full of dolls and clothes we open up whenever children come to visit us at Tonsåsen.

THROUGHOUT THE BOOK, we play the same way as when we did the photo shoots.

Imagine being little and getting to go into a house full of surprises; a house with strange objects and toys that you are allowed to rummage through, take out, and leave out without anyone telling you to pick up.

Imagine a house with antique bureaus, big chests, and old trunks that are full of hand-made clothes, dolls, and other exciting treasures that only come out into the fresh air when you come for a visit – and they can stay out for as long as you like because you are having fun playing with them. The motivation behind the knitted dolls is to make a small person who comes for a visit happy. Perhaps it is because we never had such a secret and exciting room when we were small – the kind of room you only see in films. But maybe it's because we are a little childlike ourselves and have really never let go of this dream. Our dolls are not only for children—adults with a childlike frame of mind can also enjoy them. Even if you don't play with the dolls, you can still make one for someone else. We want to give you a peek into the doll workshop, share some of our inspiration, and give you some patterns that you can build upon.

This is, in many ways, a fulfilling dream for us: finally we can bring out the childlike aspects of ourselves and play through a whole book! And now we hope we can inspire you to do the same. We want you to enjoy the doll patterns and clothes, design your own, and maybe make other people happy with what you have created. You might even make your own exciting and playful universe that a child or grandchild can explore... Or, if you are a seasoned knitter, you could even resize these miniature patterns to knit garments for children or adults.

Here is a room for playing in!
And we hope you have fun and will be happy
while you indulge!

Early in the 21st century, we had planned to publish a paper doll book. For a whole fall, we sat at home and drew many different dolls with their clothes. And then the dolls got a large and fantastic wardrobe with fashionable clothes and accessories. Unfortunately the paper doll book was never published but some of the clothes we had drawn for the dolls became actual models that we later began to design and produce for our fashion collections. This chest with paper dolls lies in our archives in our studio, and we have many times referenced these drawings for inspiration and ideas for new projects.

WE USED A BARBIE DOLL as a mannequin; she's the perfect size to simply drape fabric around. We had done this many times when we were in the design process, trying out ideas for various garments, particularly when we were designing the summer 2003 collection we called "Origami." Afterwards we made the full-size models. Some of these full-size models can still be seen at the Art Industry Museum in Oslo, in the Jubilee Exhibition on Design from 1905-2005.

WHEN ANYONE has a small company as we do, with just the two of us, you have to find the smartest solutions for getting a lot done in the simplest ways. In the past few years, we've knit many sweaters in miniature because they are quick to knit. If we have ideas for a relief stitch pattern, we can knit a sweater in an evening! This has turned out to be very clever, because we can test our ideas quickly before we begin to make the garment in an adult size.

IN SEPTEMBER 2009 we visited an exhibition of the French designer, Madeleine Vionnet (1876-1975), at the Museum of Decorative Arts in Paris. Vionnet, whose success peaked in the 1930's, was one of the most influential designers of the twentieth century. Her deceptively simple garments were created through rather complicated processes that also involved modeling and draping fabric directly on small dolls before she recreated the garment in silk or chiffon on living models. This was a fantastic exhibit with many elegant garments for inspiration. We were most fascinated and taken by all the miniature dolls exhibited together with Vionnet's designs in miniature. We studied these closely and at great length, and we talked about these dolls for a long time after we saw the exhibit. It was good to see that there were others who also used dolls as models.

IN 2010, WE VISITED THE CHATEAU DE VENDEUVRE, an eighteenth-century castle in Normandy. At the castle, we saw an exhibit of miniature furniture from the eighteenth and nineteenth centuries that the countess and owner of the castle had collected over many years. The beautiful, old furniture pieces were not toys, but precisely worked, as furniture makers would have built them to obtain a commission, or as miniature furniture that could be shown to the rich noble families who could then choose the items they wanted to order in the full size. Once again we spent most of our time at the castle studying this miniature furniture and we don't actually remember much else about our visit.

FOR A LONG TIME we've had the desire to make something childlike and playful. One day, when an eight-year-old niece visited, we gathered all the Barbie dolls with clothes that we had made. They came out of the chests and cabinets. Then we began to think about Barbie, the miniature furniture from the castle in Normandy, and the Madeleine Vionnet exhibit and we knew just what we had to do.

Of course, it had to be a doll book!

WE MADE ALL THE CLOTHES in this chest and many of the garments were also made in adult sizes. The blue and white Icelandic sweater at the center of the photo below was a best seller in men's sizes for many years. And the purple strapless evening dress that Barbie is wearing was sewn by Arne for Miss Norway for the Miss World competition in South Africa in 1996.

WE PLAYED with the idea of creating old furniture in miniature, but found out it was expensive and not a lot of fun. Instead we thought about how a child would have done this and used what we had around us: Coffee mugs turned upside down became chairs and a wineglass serves as the base of the table.

A TURTLENECK
SWEATER also
supports the neck.

THE FIRST DOLLS were made in winter 2010. We basically put a body onto a Christmas ball. The body has the shape that it does because we wanted it to look the most normal with clothes on, even dressed in layers. Because the head is so big, we designed all the sweaters and tops with wide neck openings so you could pull the clothes on from the bottom up—starting at the legs and because the dolls have big heads but thin necks, many of the garments have a high neck like a turtleneck to hold the head up.

WE WANTED the dolls to have a large wardrobe and a variety of outfits to bring out each doll's personality. So, we created Ulla, the doll with white rasta hair who wears "hen knitting" clothes. Lolita is a punk girl with a ring in her nose who goes around in black and pink clothes with skulls on them. Milton is a charming guy who likes the seaside and who has a twin sister named Milla. We have also worked with various other themes inspired by objects we have here in the house and which we used to design garments for the dolls. For example, we made a series with clothes inspired by the insects which hang on the walls in black-framed boxes. We went out into our garden and found inspiration for a series of clothes and we wrote a chapter inspired by candies and other sweets. Since we have been mostly designing sweaters inspired by Norwegian traditions during the past five years, the dolls also have five such garments.

WE HAVE KNITTED and filled dolls and made clothes for a long time now and in this book we present 44 outfits and a total of 76 different patterns for garments and accessories. We hope you will be inspired to make your own designs. On pages 197-199, you will find all the basic charts.

YARN

We used Falk from Dale of Norway for knitting the dolls. We think that Falk gives a suitable size for the dolls if you follow the instructions. This yarn isn't too tightly plied so the dolls will have smoother and softer "skin." Because Falk is machine-washable, it means the dolls won't shrink when washed in the machine. An advantage for machine-washable dolls is that the wool stuffing will felt nicely.

You can also use another yarn in suitable colors if you want as long as it works with needles U.S. size 1.5 (2.5 mm). We knit one doll with pure new wool and put it in the washing machine together with some laundry at 140°F (60°C) and it came out half as big. It then fit into the clothes we had knit for Barbie.

When it comes to yarn amounts, you'll be fine with one ball of each color for the dolls and the clothes. The only exception is the long dress with the lace coat (basic pattern 12, see page 78) you'll need 2 balls.

FALK
Sport weight, DK
Falk (100% wool; 116 yds /106 m, 50 g)

DALETTA
Fingering
Daletta (100% wool; 153 yds / 141 m, 50 g)

HUBRO
Bulky
Hubro (100% wool; 72 yds / 66 m, 100 g)

BABY ULL
Fingering
Baby Ull (100% Merino wool; 180 yds / 165 m, 50 g)

HEILO
DK /Sport
Heilo (100% wool; 108 yds / 100 m, 50 g)

LAMÉ METALLIC YARN
Fingering

FREE STYLE
Worsted
Free Style (100% wool; 87 yds / 80 m, 50 g)

ROYAL ALPAKKA
DK
Royal Alpakka (100% Alpaca; 145 yds / m, 50 g)

COLORS

We've used several colors in Falk for the skin of the dolls for diversity and variety—
we're all different! F
Natural 0020
Pale peach 3102
Sandlewood 2642
Cocoa 3072
Dark taupe 2671
Black 0090

We don't think that any of these colors is better than another. All the dolls have their own, lovely personality no matter what color you use!

THERE ARE quite a few skin and hair colors you can choose from the color card.

USE THE COLORS you like for the hair and eyelashes. Feel free to choose what you want! We have used a number of different colors from the Falk color card for the hair.

For example:

Red 4018
Dandelion 2417
Orange 3309
Mint green 7502
Black 0090
Norwegian blue 5744
Purple 5036
Pink 4415

When it comes to the clothes, we've listed the yarn we used and the color numbers that were used in the instructions for the various outfits. Of course, when you work with such small items, it is natural to go and root around in your yarn stash basket. For that reason there are outfits in the book knitted in leftover yarns and, unfortunately, we don't have any information about the yarn or color number. In any case, we list needles sizes for all the garments, so you can feel free to use the yarn from your yarn basket in the colors you want.

We've used some old buttons for the garments, use what you have on hand. We've taken buttons off worn-out clothes before discarding the garments. You never know when something will come in handy!

Buttons

Here's another place where you can choose! We have many boxes with old buttons and we have chosen a little of everything. But we have also found a good source for buttons in Norway called Hjelmtvedt and have used quite a few buttons from them for our garments. You'll find a big selection of buttons in most sewing and yarn shops or look online, there are many websites that just sell buttons. Whenever we mention in the text that we've used new buttons, they will have been purchased from Hjelmtvedt.

FILLING

AS WITH THE CHRISTMAS BALLS in our previous book, we recommend using virgin wool stuffing for the dolls. You'll need 2.5-2.8 oz (70-80 g) of wool stuffing for each doll. You can buy the wool that is usually for felting in a loose weight in most hobby or yarn stores. 100% wool will give the best results. It is important to remember that you have to stuff the doll well so that it will be sturdy. Pure wool is dirt resistant, but, if you fill the doll up completely it can also be machine washed without a problem.

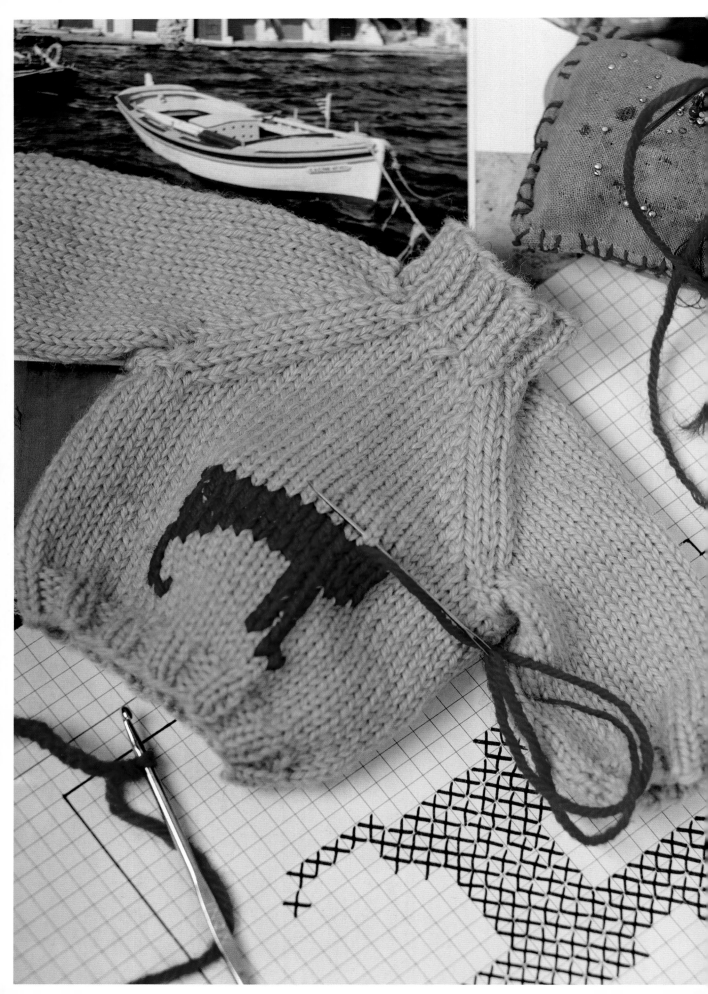

KNITTING NEEDLES AND CROCHET HOOKS

The dolls are knit with double pointed needles U.S. size 1.5 (2.5 mm). You should use smaller needles if you knit loosely so doll won't be too big and so that the wool filling won't show through. If the doll is laid flat on its back with the foot pointing to the ceiling, then it should measure 15 ¾ in (40 cm) from the heel to the top of the head. However, everyone knits differently so the length of of each knitter's doll may vary. This measurement is just an indication of the general size of the doll.

We recommend metal knitting needles for making the dolls. The reason is that the doll should be knit tightly so it will be firm and sturdy. It is not possible to knit very tightly with bamboo needles so they shouldn't be used for the dolls, although you can use bamboo needles for the garments if you like.

The gauge for our dolls is 3 stitches in ⅜ in (1 cm). It's a good idea to knit a small gauge swatch so you can check the gauge before you begin knitting the doll.

ABBREVIATIONS

BO	bind off (bind off knitwise unless otherwise instructed) (= British cast off)
ch	chain (crochet)
cm	centimeter(s)
CO	cast on
dpn	double-pointed needle(s)
g	gram(s)
in	inch(es)
k	knit

k2tog	knit 2 together
inc	Increase with lifted stitches from row below (see page 25)
mm	millimeter(s)
ndl(s)	needle(s)
p	purl
p2tog	purl 2 together
psso	pass slipped stitch over
rep	repeat
rnd(s)	round(s)
RS	right side
sc	single crochet (= British double crochet dc)

sl	slip
st(s)	stitch(es)
tbl	through back loop(s)
tr	treble crochet (= British double treble dtr)
WS	wrong side
yo	yarnover (= British yarn forward or yarn around needle)

U.S. TERM	BRITISH TERM
gauge	tension
skip	miss

Chapter 3
KNITTING AND EMBROIDERY TECHNIQUES

THIS SECTION INCLUDES step-by-step drawings to explain a little about our knitting methods and embroidery techniques. In addition to knitting the dolls and their clothes, we use various embroidery techniques for eyelashes and the mouth. We also occasionally decorate the garments with duplicate, back, lazy daisy stitches and pompoms. Later in the book we'll refer back to this chapter for any special embroidery stitches needed for a garment.

A. CASTING ON

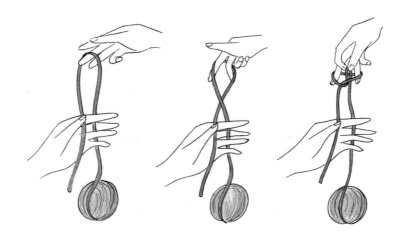

1. MAKE A SLIP KNOT LOOP.

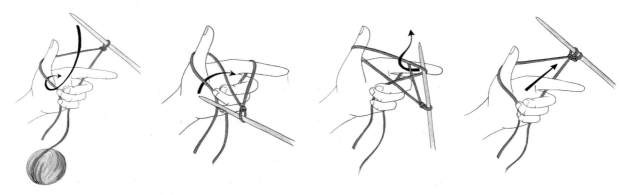

2. PUT THE LOOP ON A NEEDLE AND CAST ON THE STITCHES.

B. Increasing

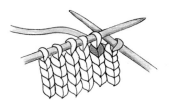 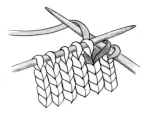 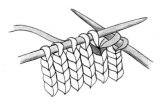

INCREASE AT THE BEGINNING of the row by picking up a stitch at the right side of the stitch below the second stitch on the needle.

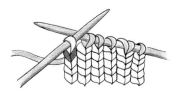  

INCREASE AT THE END of the needle by picking up a stitch on the right side of the stitch below the last stitch on the needle.

ALL INCREASES IN THE DOLLS and garments are made by lifted increases from the stitch below rather than make 1.

C. Back Stitch

2.

3.

1.

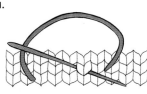 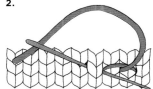 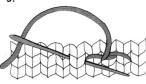

1. **WHEN YOU WORK THE FIRST STITCH,** decide how long you want to make each stitch.

2. **MAKE THE SECOND STITCH** by inserting the needle half a stitch length from the end of the first stitch and then bring the needle up at the center of the first stitch. Continue the same way to the end of the pattern.

3. **WHEN YOU MAKE THE BACK STITCHES THIS WAY,** all the stitches will be the same length. It is very important that the embroidery be worked very smoothly and that the stitches align.

D. Duplicate Stitch

1.

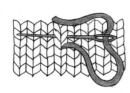

2.

3.

SOMETIMES IT IS EASIER to embroider a pattern or motif than to knit it in. If you are using only a little bit of a color in a pattern or motif it would be easier to embroider it. If the entire motif needs to be embroidered, mark off a stitch in the knitting that corresponds to a stitch in the motif.

E. Lazy Daisy Stitch

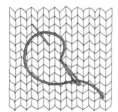
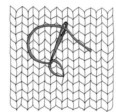
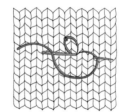
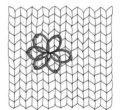

EMBROIDER THE PETALS of the flower by making large loops out from the center of the flower. On the flower jacket we made some extra stitches in another color over the petals at the inside of the flower center.

Tassels and Pompoms

Cut out two paper circles with a hole at the center for each pompom, hold the two paper circles together and wrap the yarn around them. Use a tapestry needle to help wind the yarn when it gets too tight at the center. Insert the scissors point between the two layers of paper and cut the yarn open. Tie the yarn very tightly to secure the pompom before your tear away the paper.

ADDING POMPOMS
to Siv's headband
makes it an attractive
ear warmer.

PART 1: THE DOLL'S BODY

We start by knitting the legs and working up the body. Besides the ears there are only three seams on the doll's body, between the legs and under the arms. Stuff in the wool as you knit and make sure it is evenly distributed and not clumping.

MATERIALS

2 sets of 5 dpn U.S. size 1.5 (2.5 mm)
Yarn for the body and hair: Falk.
Wool stuffing 2.8 oz (80 g)

The doll must be knitted firmly so go down a needle size if necessary. You don't want the wool stuffing to come out or show through the stitches.

RIGHT LEG

With needles U.S. 1.5 (2.5 mm), CO 8 sts. Divide sts evenly over 4 dpn = 2 sts on each needle.
Join, being careful not to twist cast-on sts.
RND 1: K8.
RND 2: *K1, inc 1, k1*; rep from * to * around.
RND 3: K12.
RND 4: *K1, inc 1, k1, inc 1, k1*; rep from * to * around.

RND 5: K20.
RND 6: *K1, inc 1, k3, inc 1, k1*; rep from * to * around.
Knit 8 rnds or ¾ in (2 cm).
Weave in yarn end at tip of toe neatly on WS and then stuff foot with wool.

HEEL

Over half of the stitches, work 8 rows back and forth in stockinette (knit 1 row, turn and purl 1 row), beginning with a knit (RS) row.

Continue by working over all 4 needles as follows:
NDL 1: K7.
NDL 2: Pick up and knit 5 sts from the side of the heel with ndl 2 and k12.
NDL 3: K7.
NDL 4: Pick up and knit 5 sts from the other side of the heel with ndl 4 and k12.

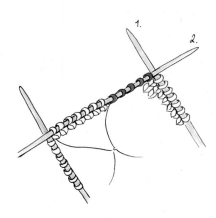

LEGS AND THIGHS

Rnd 1: K7, k2tog, k27, k2tog.
Rnd 2: Knit around.
Rnd 3: K7, k2tog, k25, k2tog.
Rnd 4: Knit around.
Rnd 5: K7, k2tog, k23, k2tog.
Rnd 6: Knit around.
Rnd 7: K7, k2tog, k21, k2tog.
Rnd 8: Knit around.
Rnd 9: K7, k2tog, k19, k2tog.
Rnd 10: Knit around.
Rnd 11: *K1, k2tog, k1, k2tog, k1*; rep from * to * around.
Rnd 12: K20.
Rnd 13: *K1, k2tog, k2*; rep from * to * around.
Rnd 14: K16.
Rnd 15: *K1, k2tog, k1*; rep from * to * around.
12 sts now remain.

Start the leg by dividing these 12 sts over 3 ndls = 4 sts per ndl and use the 4th ndl to knit with. Knit 70 rnds or 6 ¾ in (17 cm). Use a thread marker to indicate the beginning of the round. Stuff the leg with wool as you work. Use a pencil or something similar to push the wool down. Don't fill the piece all the way to the top to avoid the wool getting caught into the knitting.

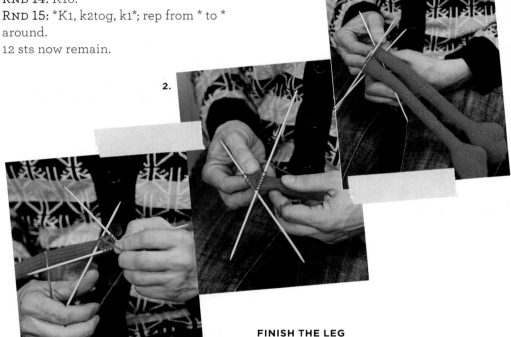

FINISH THE LEG

Rnd 1: K1, inc 1, k10, inc 1, k1.
Rnd 2: K14.
Rnd 3: K1, inc 1, k12, inc 1, k1.
Rnd 4: K16.
Rnd 5: K1, inc 1, k14, inc 1, k1.
Rnd 6: BO 2 sts, k14 (including the last st from the bind-off), BO the last 2 sts. Divide the leg sts over 2 dpn = 7 sts on each needle.

LEFT LEG

CO 8 sts onto the other set of dpn and follow the instructions for the right leg.
Finish the leg as follows:
RND 1: K5, inc 1, k2, inc 1, k5.
RND 2: K14.
RND 3: K6, inc 1, k2, inc 1, k6.
RND 4: K16.
RND 5: K7, inc 1, k2, inc 1, k7.
RND 6: K7, BO 4, k7 (including the last st from bind-off).

Divide the leg sts over 2 dpn = 7 sts on each needle.
Join the legs and knit over all sts.
Work 7 rnds or ¾ in (2 cm).
Sew the groin seam together and fill the legs with wool.

BODY AND ARMS
With a T-shirt

Change to the T-shirt color and knit 20 rnds or 1 ¾ in (4.5 cm).

RND 21: BO 2 sts, k10 (including last st from bind-off), BO 4 sts, k10 (including last st from bind-off), BO the last 2 sts. Place the 10 front sts on one needle and the 10 back sts on another needle.

BEGIN THE ARMS

CO 8 sts with arm color and U.S. 1.5 (2.5 mm) needles; divide the sts evenly over 4 dpn = 2 sts per needle.
RND 1: K8.
RND 2: K1, inc 1, k1*; rep from * to * around.
RND 3: K12.
RND 4: *K1, inc 1, k1, inc 1, k1*; rep from * to * around.
RND 5: K20.

RND 6: *K1, inc1, k3, inc1, k1*; rep from * to * around.
Knit 9 rnds or ¾ in (2 cm).
Weave the yarn end from tip of hand neatly on WS.

RND 16: *K1, k2tog, k1, k2tog, k1*; rep from * to * around.
RND 17: K20.
RND 18: *K1, k2tog, k2*; rep from * to * around.
RND 19: K16.
RND 20: *K1, k2tog, k1*; rep from * to * around.
Divide remaining 12 sts over 3 dpn = 4 sts on each needle.

Continue by knitting 35 rnds or 3 ¼ in (8 cm) with skin color. Fill the arm with wool as you work. Change to T-shirt color and knit 5 rnds.
Last rnd: BO 2 sts, k8 (including the last st from bind-off), BO the last 2 sts. Put the 8 sts onto 1 dpn.
Make the other arm the same way.

We made several different designs for knitting the T-shirts and pants directly on the body—we have both single color T-shirts, and T-shirts with patterns as well as single-colored pants and pants with stripes. You'll find charts and more information about undergarments in **Chapter 6**.

KNITTING THE BODY AND ARMS TOGETHER

RAGLAN SHAPING:

Divide the sts over 4 dpn, with 8 sts for each arm and 10 sts for the front of the body and 10 sts for the back.

RND 1: K10 for back, k8 for one arm, k10 for front and k8 for the other arm.

RND 2: Back: K1, k2tog, k4, k2tog, k1; arm: k8; front: k1, k2tog, k4, k2tog, k1; arm: k8.

RND 3: K32.

RND 4: *K1, k2tog, k2, k2tog, k1*; rep from * to * around.

RND 5: K24.

RND 6 (KNIT WITH T-SHIRT COLOR): *K1, k2tog, k2tog, k1*; rep from * to * around. Knit the last rnd in the T-shirt color.

Seam the armholes and weave in all ends on WS.

Fill with wool.

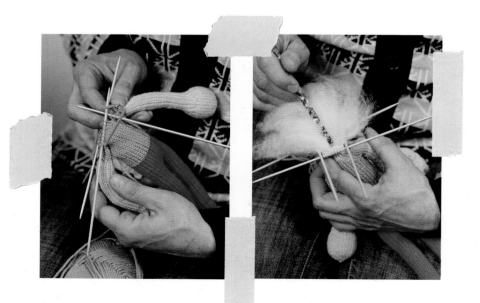

MILTON RELAXING on a cruise.

DIEGO RIVERA'S 1949 PAINTING of Pita Amor inspired the eyes for our dolls. A pretty woman but a little stiff looking. We tried various approaches until we decided on knitted eyes. We tried buttons, ready-made eyes from the hobby shop, and embroidered eyes but they didn't give us the expression we were after.

PART 2: EYES, NOSE, MOUTH, AND HAIR

Now it's time to add facial expression and hair to the doll. Once the eyes are made, everything changes. Many children put eyes on a sock so it becomes a living creature. There's no turning back now, once the hair and mouth are added the doll comes to life.

NECK AND HEAD
RND 1: K16.
RND 2: *K1, k2tog, k1*; rep from * to * around.
RNDS 3-8: Knit.
RND 9: *K1, inc 1, k1, inc 1, k1*; rep from * to * around.
RND 10: K20.
RND 11: *K1, inc 1, k3, inc 1, k1*; rep from * to * around.
RND 12: K28.
RND 13: *K1, inc 1, k5, inc 1, k1*; rep from * to * around.
RND 14: K36.
RND 15: *K1, inc 1, k7, inc 1, k1*; rep from * to * around.
RND 16: K44.
RND 17: *K1, inc 1, k9, inc 1, k1*; rep from * to * around.
RND 18: K52.
RND 19: *K1, inc 1, k11, inc 1, k1*; rep from * to * around.
RND 20: K60.
RND 21: *K1, inc 1, k13, inc 1, k1*; rep from * to * around.
RNDS 22-24: Knit.

NOSE
RND 25: Knit the nose as follows:

NDL 1: K17.
NDL 2: K17.
NDL 3: K8, inc 5 by working (k1, p1, k1, p1, k1) into the 9th st.
Turn and purl the 5 sts.
Turn and k5.
Turn and p5.
Finish nose on RS by knitting the 5 sts on right ndl, and then pass the 2nd st over the 1st st; do the same with the 3rd, 4th, and then the 5th st. Pull the sts together and end with k8.
NDL 4: K17.

RND 26: K68.

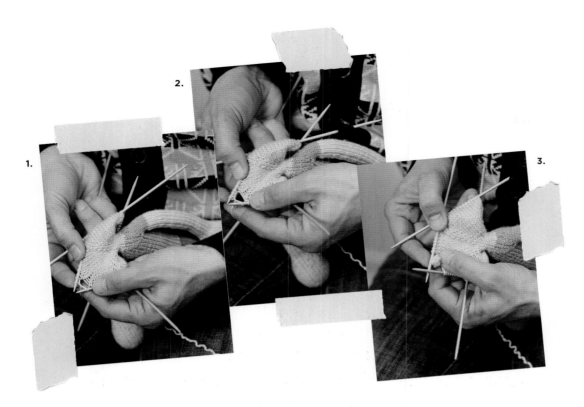

BEGIN THE HOLES FOR THE EYES

Rnd 27:
Ndl 1: K17.
Ndl 2: K17.
Ndl 3: K2, BO 4, k5 (including the last st from bind-off), BO 4 sts, k2 (including last st from bind-off).
Ndl 4: K17.

Rnd 28:
Ndl 1: K17.
Ndl 2: K17.
Ndl 3: K2, CO 4, k5, CO 4, k2.
Ndl 4: K17.

Rnds 29-34: Knit.
Rnd 35: *K1, k2tog, k11, k2tog, k1*; rep form * to * around.
Rnd 36: K60.
Rnd 37: *K1, k2tog, k9, k2tog, k1*; rep form * to * around.
Rnd 38: K52.

Now prepare the eyes before you continue knitting:

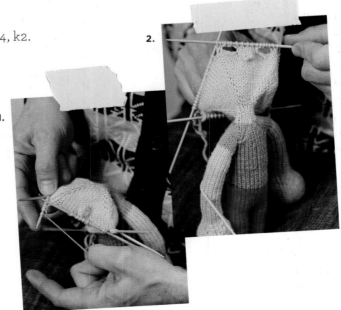

SOMETIMES IT IS EASIER to sew on buttons for the eyes instead of knitting them. This is the only doll we knit with pure new wool. She was washed in 140ºF (60ºC) water and came out half as large. She is wearing Barbie's sweater and pants (the patterns for these garments are not in the book).

If you are making a doll for a young child, don't use buttons or other types of eyes that can be pulled off. Knitted or embroidered eyes are the safest if there are young children in the house. The eyes immediately give life and personality to the doll.

KNITTED EYES

With desired eye color and dpn U.S. 1.5 (2.5 mm), CO 8 sts.

RND 1: With white, k8 sts on 1 needle. Cut eye color and work with white only.
RND 2: Divide the 8 sts over 4 dpn = 2 sts on each ndl. Work *K1, inc 1, k1* on each of the 4 needles.
RND 3: K12.
RND 4: *K1, inc 1, k1, inc 1, k1*; rep from * to * around.
RND 5: K20.
BO. Make another eye the same way. Weave in ends on WS and carefully steam press the eyes.

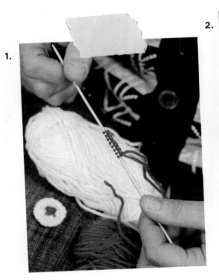

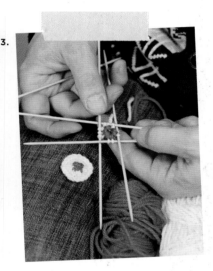

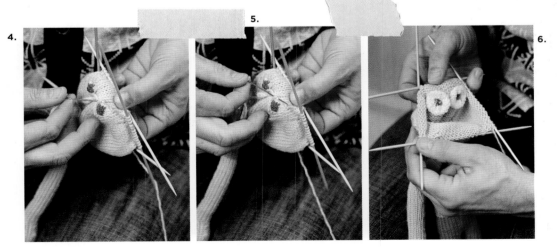

POSITION THE EYES BEHIND THE HOLES, pressing them a little outwards so that the white pupils are somewhat rounded in the eye sockets. Decide in which direction the doll will be looking. Sew in the eyes with skin color yarn.

FINISH HEAD

RND 39: *K1, k2tog, k7, k2tog, k1*; rep from * to * around.
RND 40: K44.
RND 41: *K1, k2tog, k5, k2tog, k1*; rep from * to * around.
RND 42: K36.
Check to make sure that the throat is filled properly. If it is empty, fill it up well so that the head won't hang down when the doll is finished.

RND 43: *K1, k2tog, k3, k2tog, k1*; rep from * to * around.
RND 44: K28.
RND 45: *K1, k2tog, k1, k2tog, k1*; rep from * to * around.
RND 46: K20.
RND 47: *K1, k2tog, k2*; rep from * to * around.
RND 48: K16.
RND 49: *K1, k2tog, k1*; rep from * to * around.
Cut yarn and pull end through remaining 12 sts.

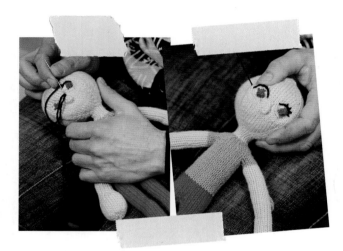

FILL THE HEAD WITH WOOL and sew the hole at the top together. Embroider on the eyelashes with back stitch and embroider on straight stitches for longer eyelashes if you like. We are all different!

MOUTH

EMBROIDER THE MOUTH on with back stitches. See the section on how to embroider back stitches in Chapter 3, page 25.

AGATHA HAS black embroidered eyelashes while Kaja has lovely red lashes.

HAIR

USE SPECIAL COLORS FOR THE HAIR so each of the dolls will have its own personality.
If you are going to machine wash the doll, it is important that you knot the hair in well
so that it doesn't felt—unless you want a doll with Rasta hair, like Ulla.
If you want that effect, use a pure wool yarn so that the hair will felt and clump after a
few cycles in the washer. Ulla's hair is made with wool embroidery yarn that we
had lying around. Arne and Milton's curly hair came from yarn that we unraveled
from an old sweater.

WE BEGIN BY marking the hairline around the head. Cut the yarn to desired length. We usually wrap the yarn around an A4 notebook (11 ½ x 8 ¼ in) for the right length hair. Fold the yarn lengths at the center and use a crochet hook to draw the yarn through a stitch. Pull the ends through the yarn loop and tighten.

WE USED one or two strands in each hair length for thinner or thicker hair.

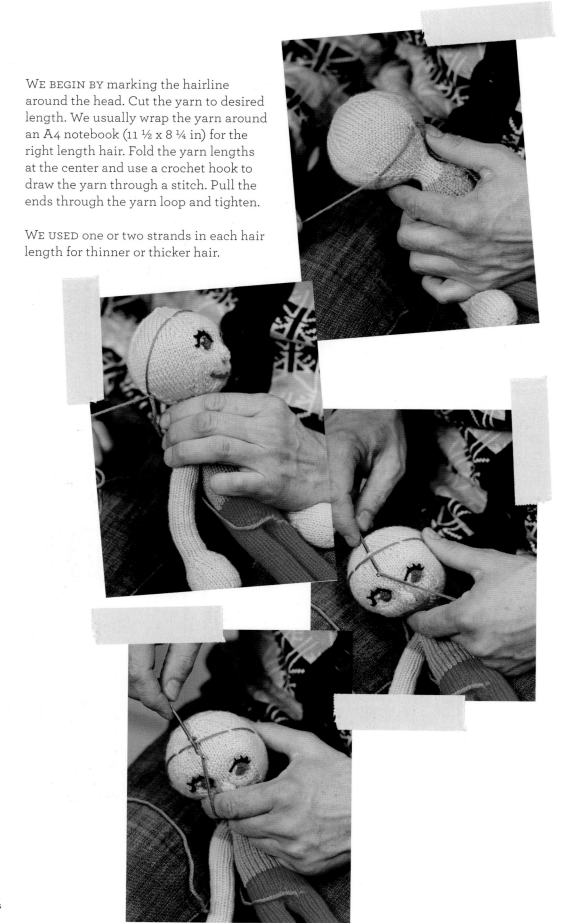

WHEN YOU'VE ADDED HAIR all around the head along the marked hairline, you might also decide to section off the area between the decreases at the front and add more lengths of hair in that section. Take all the hair, pull it up and make a ponytail attached to the highest point. If you want, you can add in short yarn lengths for bangs.

ALTERNATELY, you can continue to attach hair at various points around the whole head. This means a lot of hair but you'll have more options for making fun hairstyles and cutting hair to different lengths than if you only make the version with the ponytail.

SIV ONLY HAS HAIR around the hairline. We pulled the hair up into a ponytail. The doll with green hair has thicker hair because we attached lengths of yarn at various points around the head.

Shirley *

Maja

SIV

Milla

Beate ***

Arne

Sissel

Agnethe

KRYSTEL

MILTON

Ulla

Kaja

Vivian

LOLITA

Carlos

Chapter 6

Undergarments

Each doll can be knit in a skin color if you want but, because the doll is so thin, it is a little crazy to make underclothes for it. For that reason, we decided to make the undergarments directly on the body. Milton has a red "speedo" swimsuit. Siv, Kaja, Sissel and Agnethe are wearing patterned T-shirts and Sissel and Agnethe also have striped pants. The rest of the dolls have solid color T-shirts and pants. It was fun putting together color combinations for the underclothes for the dolls and it made the job of knitting them all the more pleasing, even if the patterns on the T-shirts were a bit complicated to knit.

Here are some tips for knitting the undergarments. The empty basic outline for the T-shirt shows half of the body and the whole sleeve. The block of squares marked off on the bottom of the chart falls at the place on the body where you knit the legs together.

FOR MILTON'S SWIMSUIT we started knitting the legs together by changing to red 4018 and knitting 7 rounds before changing back to the skin color. We later sewed the legs together with red, joining the swimsuit.

MilTon

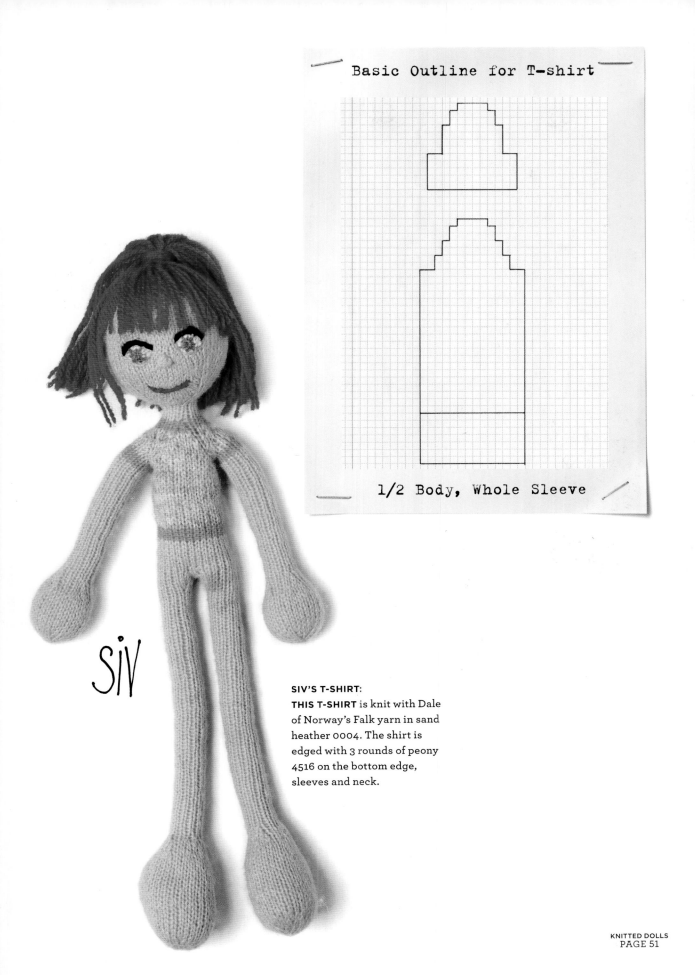

Basic Outline for T-shirt

1/2 Body, Whole Sleeve

SIV

SIV'S T-SHIRT:
THIS T-SHIRT is knit with Dale of Norway's Falk yarn in sand heather 0004. The shirt is edged with 3 rounds of peony 4516 on the bottom edge, sleeves and neck.

1/2 Body

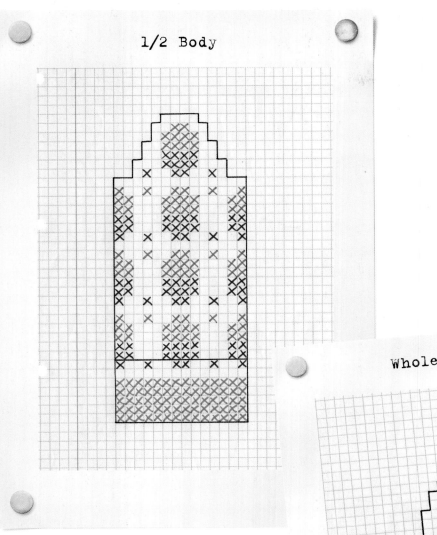

Whole Sleeve

THIS T-SHIRT is two rounds longer at the bottom. When designing your own T-shirt, add pattern stitches below the marked line for the bottom edge of the shirt if necessary to complete the pattern motif. The sleeve begins 3 rounds below the marked line for the sleeve edging. See page 51.

MATERIALS:
Dale of Norway, Falk
Natural 0020
Purple 5036
Red 4018

AGNETHE'S T-SHIRT WITH HEARTS AND SISSEL'S AND AGNETHE'S STRIPED PANTS.

Agnethe

Sissel

SISSEL'S T-SHIRT
MATERIALS:
Dale of Norway, Falk
Red 4018

SISSEL'S STRIPED PANTS
MATERIALS:
Dale of Norway, Falk
Natural 0020
Dark turquoise 6215
Sand heather 0004

Stripe Repeat: *3 white, 1 turquoise, 2 gray, 1 turquoise*; rep from * to *.

AGNETHE'S T-SHIRT WITH HEARTS:
MATERIALS:
Dale of Norway, Falk
Natural 0020
Cyclamen 4536

AGNETHE'S PANTS
MATERIALS:
Dale of Norway, Falk
Norwegian blue 5744
Ice blue 5822

Begin with Norwegian blue and knit 3

rounds in each color. Make the heel with
Norwegian blue.

If you are knitting striped pants, adjust
the length of the T-shirt if you want the
stripes to "go up" so they will finish at the
right color in the pattern sequence.

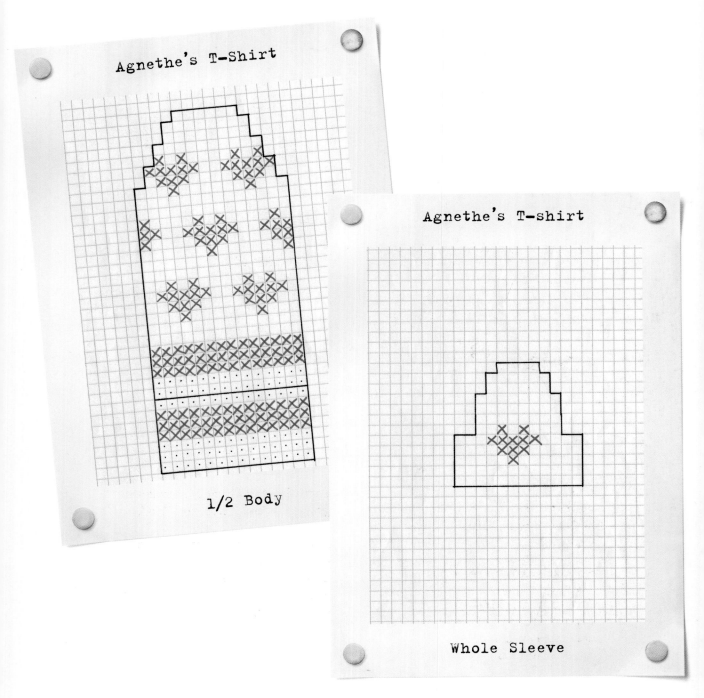

"BUT I HAVE NOTHING TO WEAR!"
Agnethe

AN OLD MEDICINE CABINET serves as a clothes closet. **WHY NOT DRESS UP** the clothes with old chains of beads.

INSTRUCTIONS FOR THE BASIC GARMENTS

We've written some basic instructions for the garments in this book. We have tried to make them as easy as possible and with small variations that can be the basis for many different garments. Knit a garter stitch edge instead of ribbing to give sweaters and jackets a totally new look. The basic garments have different patterns for the various themes and of course different colors and buttons—it's the little things that make it fun to dress up your doll! Once you've learned how to construct the basic garment, following the charts will be easier. The clothes will vary in size from knitter to knitter and depending on what yarn you use. We let you know what yarns we used for all the simple models but some of the garments were knit with leftovers and we no longer remember the name of the yarn. We have kept to needles U.S. sizes 1.5 and 2.5 (2.5 and 3 mm) or U.S. 7 and 8 (4.5 and 5 mm). You'll soon realize when you must finish a garment before the pattern ends or make it a little longer. It is impossible to control everything since we all knit differently. But if you knit the doll yourself, the clothes should fit it. Where we show a number of inches/centimeters of knitting instead of a number of rounds, you should check the length on the doll while you knit so that the garment will fit.

"MIRROR MIRROR ON THE WALL, WHO'S THE FAIREST OF THEM ALL?"

A classic sweater for a cold winter day!

By varying the ribbed edges, neck and length of the body and sleeves you can get many different designs from the same pattern. Later in the book, we'll show some basic patterns and together with the designs you'll get graph paper and explanations for other options for the ribbed edges and neck openings. The sweater is loose fitting so if you knit loosely, we recommend that you go down a needle size. You can also vary the size of the sweater by changing yarn.

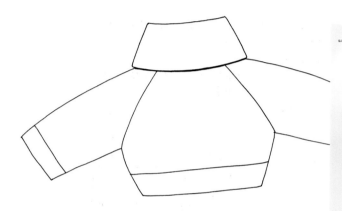

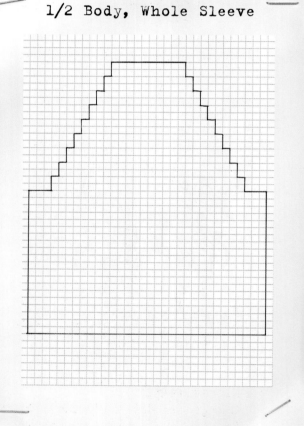

1/2 Body, Whole Sleeve

MATERIALS

1 set of 5 dpn U.S. sizes 1.5 and 2.5 (2.5 and 3 mm).
Yarn suitable for these needle sizes, for example, Dale of Norway Falk, Daletta, Heilo, Babyull. The specific yarn you choose will affect the garment sizing. A Babyull sweater will be a little smaller and softer than one knit with Falk.

BODY

With smaller needles, CO 48 sts and divide them over 4 dpn = 12 sts on each ndl.
RNDS 1-5: Work in k2, p2 rib.
RND 6: Change to larger needles and work *K3, inc 1*; rep from * to * around.
Knit 21 rnds for the longer sweater or 9 rnds for a short one.
RND 28 (OR RND 16): BO 3, k26 (including the last st from bind-off), BO 6, k26 (including last st from bind-off), BO 3.

Divide the sts for front and back onto separate needles = 26 sts on each needle.

SLEEVES: With smaller needles, CO 24 sts and divide onto 4 dpn = 6 sts on each needle.

RNDS 1-5: Work in k2, p2 rib.

RND 6: Change to larger needles and work *K3, inc 1*; rep from * to * around. Knit 21 rnds for long sleeves or 9 rnds for short sleeves.

RND 28 (OR RND 16): BO 3, k26 (including the last st from bind-off), BO 3.

Join body and sleeves:

RND 29: K26 for back, k26 for sleeve, k26 for front, k26 for sleeve.

RND 30: *K1, k2tog, k20, k2tog, k1*; rep from * to * around.

RND 31: K96.

RND 32: *K1, k2tog, k18, k2tog, k1*; rep from * to * around.

RND 33: K88.

RND 34: *K1, k2tog, k16, k2tog, k1*; rep from * to * around.

RND 35: K80.

RND 36: *K1, k2tog, k14, k2tog, k1*; rep from * to * around.

RND 37: K72.

RND 38: *K1, k2tog, k12, k2tog, k1*; rep from * to * around.

RND 39: K64.

RND 40: *K1, k2tog, k10, k2tog, k1*; rep from * to * around.

RND 41: K56.

RND 42: *K1, k2tog, k8, k2tog, k1*; rep from * to * around.

RND 43: K48.

RND 44: *K1, k2tog, k6, k2tog, k1*; rep from * to * around.

RND 45: K40.

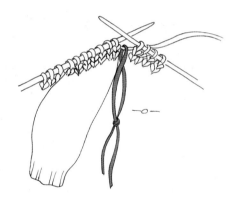

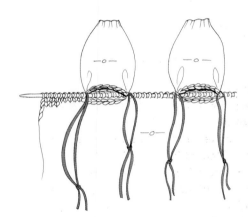

TIP: Place a marker at each intersection of the body and sleeves so that you will know exactly where to place the raglan decreases.

ALTERNATIVE 1:
Change to smaller needles and work
RND 46: *K2, p2*; rep from * to * around.
Bind off.

ALTERNATIVE 2:
K2tog, yo, p2; rep from * to * around.
Work 8 rnds k2, p2 rib.
Bind off.
Crochet a cord and pull through the row of yarnover holes.

Make 2 small pompoms and tie one to each end of the crocheted cord.

ALTERNATIVE 3: Work 10 rnds k2, p2 rib and then BO.

FINISHING:
Sew the underarm seams. Weave in all ends on WS. Carefully steam press garment except for the ribbing and neck.

Some tips for knitting the sweaters

When attaching the sleeves to the body, first pin baste the sleeves in to make the work easier.

As you knit, check the length of the body and sleeves to make sure they fit your doll. You might need to eliminate a few rows so the sweater will fit well, or perhaps you want to have a longer body but shorter sleeves.

Knitting tips for striped sweaters

The chart for the sleeves shows the whole sleeve; the chart for the body only shows half of the body; the front and back are knit alike.

When the last row on the body is not the same color as the ribbing on the neck, knit an extra round, knit the same color as the neck before beginning the ribbing. That way you'll have a smooth transition between the body and neck without visible purl stitches.

The shaping on the sleeves should occur at the same place in the color sequence on both the body and sleeves so that the colors will match in the raglan shaping. The length of the sweater will also be dependent on how the stripes are placed on the body and sleeves.

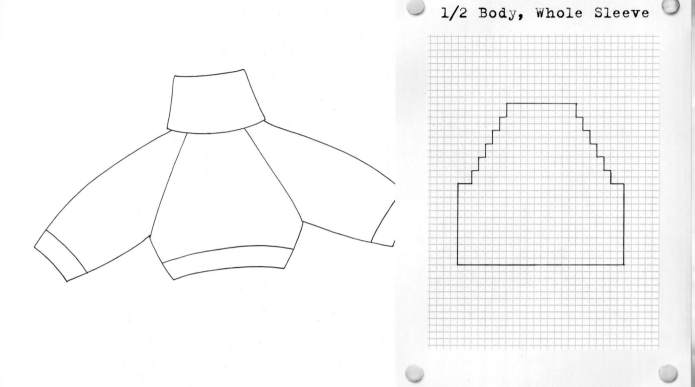

1/2 Body, Whole Sleeve

MATERIALS

1 set of 5 dpn U.S. sizes 1.5 and 2.5 (2.5 and 3 mm).

Yarn suitable for needle sizes, such as Falk, Daletta, Heilo, Babyull. Your choice of yarn will make a slight difference in the garment. For example, a Babyull sweater will be a little smaller and softer than a sweater knit with Falk.

This sweater fits snugly so you can dress the doll in layers. If you want to use the sweater as the main garment, you'll have a stylish, fitting sweater!

As you knit, check the length of the body and sleeves to make sure they fit your doll. You might need to eliminate a few rows so that the sweater will fit well, or perhaps you want to have a longer body but shorter sleeves.

BODY

With smaller needles, CO 48 sts and divide evenly over 4 dpn = 12 sts on each needle. Join, being careful not to twist cast-on row.

Work 5 rnds k2, p2 rib.

Change to larger needles and knit 12 rnds.

RND 13: BO 2 sts, k20 (including the last st from bind-off), BO 4, k20 (including the last st from bind-off), BO 2.

SLEEVES

With smaller needles, CO 24 sts and divide evenly over 4 dpn = 6 sts on each needle.

Work 5 rnds k2, p2 rib.

Change to larger needles and knit 24 rnds.

RND 25: BO 2, k20 (including last st from bind-off), BO 2.

Join body and sleeves: Place 20 sts for the back and 20 sts for the front each on separate needles.

RND 1: K20 for back, k20 for left sleeve, k20 for front, k20 for right sleeve.
RND 2: *K1, k2tog, k14, k2tog, k1*; rep from * to * around.
RND 3: K72.
RND 4: *K1, k2tog, k12, k2tog, k1*; rep from * to * around.
RND 5: K64.
RND 6: *K1, k2tog, k10, k2tog, k1*; rep from * to * around.

RND 7: K56.
RND 8: *K1, k2tog, k8, k2tog, k1*; rep from * to * around.
RND 9: K48.
RND 10: *K1, k2tog, k6, k2tog, k1*; rep from * to * around.
RND 11: K40.
Change to smaller needles and work 30 rnds k2, p2 rib.

Bind off. Sew underarm seams and weave in all ends on WS. Carefully steam press garment except for ribbed edges.

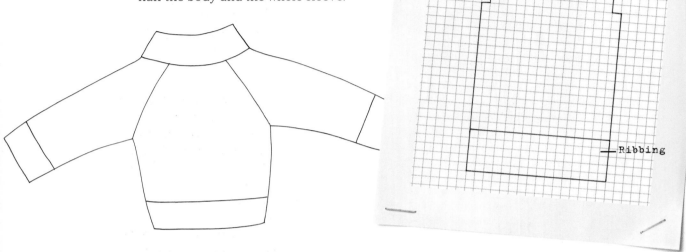

1/2 Body, Whole Sleeve

Ribbing

Ribbing

BASIC PATTERN 4: THICK SWEATER

We used Freestyle for knitting this lovely sweater for hiking in the woods and fields or up in the mountains. This is a quick sweater to knit and you can make several of them in an evening! The chart shows half the body and the whole sleeve.

MATERIALS
1 set of 5 dpn U.S. sizes 7 and 8 (4.5 and 5 mm).
Yarn: Freestyle

BODY
With smaller needles, CO 32 sts and divide evenly onto 4 dpn = 8 sts on each needle. Join, being careful not to twist cast-on row. Work 5 rnds k2, p2 rib.

Change to larger needles and knit around for 2 ½ in (6 cm) or to desired length to underarm.

Shaping at underarm: BO 1 st, k14 (including last st from bind-off), BO 2, k14, (including last st from bind-off), BO 1. Put body sts onto 2 dpn = 14 sts for front and 14 sts for back.

SLEEVES
With smaller needles, CO 16 sts. Work 5 rnds k2, p2 rib. Change to larger needles and knit for 2 ½ in (6 cm) or desired length.

Underarm shaping: BO 1 st, k14 (including last st from bind-off), BO 1.
Make the other sleeve the same way and put sts of each sleeve on a separate needle.

Join the body and sleeves:
RND 1: Knit.
RND 2: *K1, k2tog, k8, k2tog, k1*; rep from * to * around.
RND 3: Knit.
RND 4: *K1, k2tog, k6, k2tog, k1*; rep from * to * around.
RND 5: Knit.
RND 6: *K1, k2tog, k4, k2tog, k1*; rep from * to * around.
RND 7: Knit.
RND 8: *K1, k2tog, k2, k2tog, k1*; rep from * to * around.
RND 9: Knit.
Change to smaller needles and work 5 rnds (or desired length) in k2, p2 rib for neck.

Bind off. Sew underarm seams and weave in all ends on WS. Carefully steam press garment except for ribbed edges.

A jaunty and easy skirt. We have chosen to knit it in the length given but you can knit more or fewer rows if you want a longer or shorter variation of the skirt.

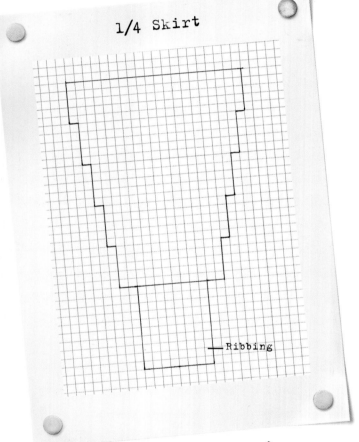

MATERIALS

1 set of 5 dpn U.S. sizes 1.5 and 2.5 (2.5 and 3 mm)
Yarn: Falk, Daletta, Babyull, or yarn suitable for given needle sizes.

With smaller needles, CO 32 sts and divide evenly over 4 dpn = 8 sts on each needle. Join, being careful not to twist cast-on row. Work 10 rnds k2, p2 rib. Change to larger needles.
Next rnd: *K2, inc 1*; rep from * to * around.
Continue knitting and increase on every 5th rnd by starting each needle with k1, inc 1 and ending each needle with inc 1, k1 (see page 25).

Increase until you have 20 sts on each needle and then knit 4 more rounds after the last increase rnd. The skirt has a variety of edgings which are explained for each individual skirt.

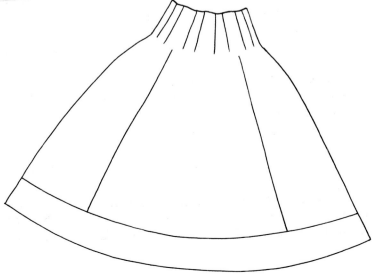

A ballerina skirt for chic and snappy dolls who want to twirl around and dance!

MATERIALS

1 set of 5 dpn U.S. sizes 1.5 and 2.5 (2.5 and 3 mm); crochet hook U.S. size C or D (3 mm)

With smaller needles, CO 32 sts and divide sts evenly over 4 dpn = 8 sts on each needle. Join, being careful not to twist cast-on row. Work 10 rnds in k2, p2 rib.

RND 11: Change to larger needles; *k2, inc 1*; rep from * to * around.
RND 12: K48.
RND 13: *K1, inc 1, k10, inc 1, k1*; rep from * to * around.
RND 14: K56.
RND 15: *K1, inc 1, k12, inc 1, k1*; rep from * to * around.
RND 16: K64.
RND 17: *K1, inc 1, k14, inc 1, k1*; rep from * to * around.
RND 18: K72.

RND 19: *K1, inc 1, k16, inc 1, k1*; rep from * to * around.
RND 20: K80.
RND 21: *K1, inc 1, k18, inc 1, k1*; rep from * to * around.
RND 22: K88.
RND 23: *K1, inc 1, k20, inc 1, k1*; rep from * to * around.
RND 24: K96.
RND 25: *K2, inc 1*; rep from * to * around.
Knit 9 rnds.
BO and then, with desired color, work 1 sc into 1st bound-off st.
Continue crocheting: *ch 4, 1 sc in the 4th ch from hook*; rep from * to * around.
Next rnd: Work 5 sc in each chain loop around; end with 1 sl st into first sc.

Cut yarn, weave in ends on WS, and carefully steam press skirt.

A classic design that can vary in length and transform entirely by being made into shorts.

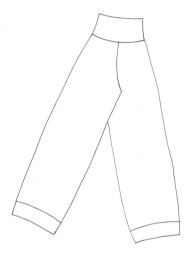

MATERIALS

1 set of 5 dpn U.S. sizes 1.5 and 2.5 (2.5 and 3 mm)
Yarn appropriate for needles, such as Falk.

Make each leg the same way:

With smaller needles, CO 36 sts and divide evenly over 4 dpn = 9 sts on each needle. Join, being careful not to twist cast-on row.
Work 7 rnds in garter st as follows:
Rnds 1, 3, 5, 7: Purl
Rnds 2, 4, 6: Knit

Change to larger needles and knit until leg is desired length. For example 5 ¼ in (13 cm) on the green pants.

Finish the leg by binding off the first 4 and last 4 sts of the round. Make the other leg the same way and then join them:

Beginning at center back and the doll's left pant leg:

RND 1: K56.
Shape center front and center back:
RND 2: K1, k2tog, k22, k2tog, k2, k2tog, k22, k2tog, k1.
RND 3: K52.
RND 4: K1, k2tog, k20, k2tog, k2, k2tog, k20, k2tog, k1.
RND 5: K48.
RND 6: K1, k2tog, k18, k2tog, k2, k2tog, k18, k2tog, k1.
RND 7: K44.
RND 8: K1, k2tog, k16, k2tog, k2, k2tog, k16, k2tog, k1.
RND 9: K40.
RND 10: K1, k2tog, k14, k2tog, k2, k2tog, k14, k2tog, k1.
RND 11: K36.
RND 12: K1, k2tog, k12, k2tog, k2, k2tog, k12, k2tog, k1.
RND 13: K32.

Change to smaller needles and work 10 rnds k2, p2 rib.

BO. Sew seam between the legs and weave in all ends on WS. Carefully steam press the pants except for the ribbing.

MATERIALS

1 set of 5 dpn U.S. sizes 1.5 and 2.5
(2.5 and 3 mm)
Yarn appropriate for needles, such as
Falk or Heilo
2 small buttons

MAKE EACH LEG THE SAME WAY:

With smaller needles, CO 36 sts and
divide evenly over 4 dpn = 9 sts on each
needle. Join, being careful not to twist
cast-on row.

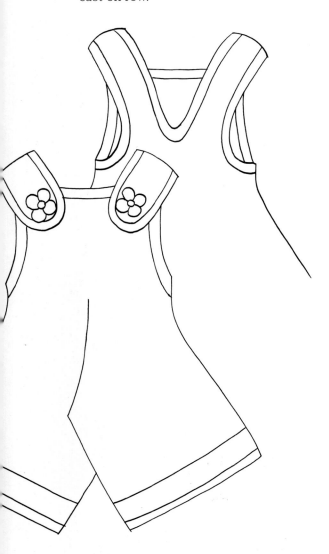

GARTER STITCH EDGING ON THE LEGS:

RND 1: Purl.
RND 2: Knit.
RND 3: Purl.
RND 4: Knit.
RND 5: Purl.

Change to larger needles and knit around
for 2 in (5 cm) to the shaping.
Continue, working through Rnd 13 following basic pants instructions 7A on
page 69.

FRONT, BIB

RND 14: K8.
Turn work and p16. Continue working
back and forth with knit on RS and purl
on WS until bib is 2 in (5 cm) long.

BACK

Row 1: K1 k2tog, k10, k2tog, k1.
Row 2: Purl.
Row 3: K1, k2tog, k8, k2tog, k1.
Row 4: Purl.
Row 5: K1, k2tog, k6, k2tog, k1.
Row 6: Purl.
Row 7: K1, k2tog, k4, k2tog, k1.
Row 8: Purl.

Make the straps with 4 sts for each:
Work back and forth in stockinette until
strap is 2 ¾ in (7 cm) long.

Work a crocheted edging around the
opening of the pant legs and around the
neck opening and straps; crochet buttonholes. Weave in ends in WS and carefully
steam press overalls. Sew on buttons.

These pants are close fitting so you have to work a little harder to pull them on the doll.

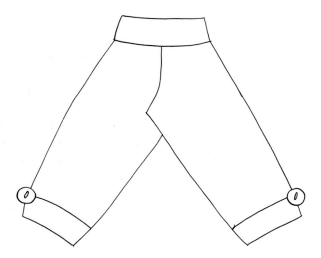

MATERIALS

1 set of 5 dpn U.S. sizes 1.5 and 2.5 (2.5 and 3 mm)
Crochet hook U.S. size C or D (3 mm)
Yarn appropriate for needles, such as Heilo or Falk
2 small buttons for the legs

LEG: With 2 of smaller dpn, CO 16 sts. Work back and forth in garter st for 5 rows.

Change to 2 of the larger dpn:
Row 6: Sl 1, k1, inc 1, *k2, inc 1*; rep from * to * until 2 sts remain and end inc 1, k1.
Row 7: P24.
Row 8: K24.
Row 9: P24.
Row 10: K24.

Now divide the sts over 4 dpn = 6 sts on each needle. Knit 20 rounds or until leg is desired length.
RND 31: K9, BO 6, k9 (including last st from bind-off). Divide leg sts over 2 dpn = 9 sts on each needle.

Make the other leg the same way with Rows 1-31.
RND 32: With leg sts divided over 4 dpn (9 sts on each needle), knit around.
RND 33: K6, k2tog, k2, k2tog, k12, k2tog, k2, k2tog, k6.
RND 34: Knit.
RND 35: K5, k2tog, k2, k2tog, k10, k2tog, k2, k2tog, k5.
RND 36: Knit.
RND 37: K4, k2tog, k2, k2tog, k8, k2tog, k2, k2tog, k4.
RND 38: Knit.

Change to smaller needles and work 5 rnds in k2, p2 rib.

Bind off and weave in ends on WS. Work sc along slit at bottom of each leg, crocheting a button loop on the front: ch 4 at lower edge of front and work 1 sc in 3rd ch from hook. Turn and work 5 sc into loop. Cut yarn and finish off.

Carefully steam press pants and sew on buttons.

This garment is perfect for a pajama party, worn as a snowsuit, or a jumpsuit. If you knit it in olive green, it will be the perfect outfit to go jeeping.

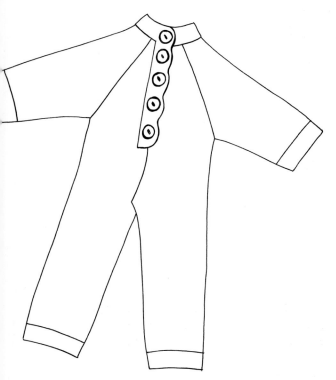

BO the first 3 and last 3 sts of the round. Divide leg sts onto 2 dpn = 15 sts on each needle.
Make the other leg the same way.

Join the legs, beginning at right leg of doll, knit across sts of front, place marker and continue around, working in stockinette for 1 ¼ in (3 cm).

Move the marker to center front and begin working from this point. Work back and forth in stockinette for 1 ½ in (4 cm). Begin all rows with k3 for the button bands.

Shape armholes on RS:
K12, BO 6, k24 (including last st from bind-off), BO 6, k12 (including last st from bind-off).

SLEEVES

With smaller needles, CO 36 sts and divide evenly over 4 dpn = 9 sts on each needle. Join, being careful not to twist cast-on row. Work 5 rnds k2, p2 rib.

Change to larger needles and knit 20 rnds or desired sleeve length.

RND 21: BO 3, k30 (including last st from bind-off), BO 3.

Join body and sleeves:
Beginning on WS with 1 purl row, begin raglan shaping on RS. Don't forget to knit 3 at the beginning and end of each row for button bands. Work raglan shaping until 5 sts remain on each front.

MATERIALS

1 set of 5 dpn U.S. sizes 1.5 and 2.5 (2.5 and 3 mm)
Crochet hook U.S. size C or D (3 mm)
Yarn appropriate for needles, such as Falk, Heilo, Daletta, or Babyull
5 small buttons

LEG

With smaller needles, CO 36 sts and divide evenly over 4 dpn = 9 sts on each needle. Join, being careful not to twist cast-on row. Work 5 rnds k2, p2 rib.

Change to larger needles and knit around for 6 ¾ in (17 cm) or desired length.

RAGLAN SHAPING

Row 1:
LEFT FRONT: K3, p9.
LEFT SLEEVE: P30.
BACK: P24.
RIGHT SLEEVE: P30.
RIGHT FRONT: P9, k3.

Row 2:
RIGHT FRONT: K9, k2tog, k1.
RIGHT SLEEVE: K1, k2tog, k24, k2tog, k1.
BACK: K1, k2tog, k18, k2tog, k1.
LEFT SLEEVE: K1, k2tog, k24, k2tog, k1.
LEFT FRONT: K1, k2tog, k9.

Row 3:
LEFT FRONT: K3, p8.
LEFT SLEEVE: P28.
BACK: P22.
RIGHT SLEEVE: P28.
RIGHT FRONT: P8, k3.

Row 4:
RIGHT FRONT: K8, k2tog, k1.
RIGHT SLEEVE: K1, k2tog, k22, k2tog, k1.
BACK: K1, k2tog, k16, k2tog, k1.
LEFT SLEEVE: K1, k2tog, k22, k2tog, k1.
LEFT FRONT: K1, k2tog, k8.

Row 5:
LEFT FRONT: K3, p7.
LEFT SLEEVE: P26.
BACK: P20.
RIGHT SLEEVE: P26.
RIGHT FRONT: P7, k3.

Row 6:
RIGHT FRONT: K7, k2tog, k1.
RIGHT SLEEVE: K1, k2tog, k20, k2tog, k1.
BACK: K1, k2tog, k14, k2tog, k1.
LEFT SLEEVE: K1, k2tog, k20, k2tog, k1.
LEFT FRONT: K1, k2tog, k7.

Row 7:
LEFT FRONT: K3, p6.
LEFT SLEEVE: P24.
BACK: P18.
RIGHT SLEEVE: P24.
RIGHT FRONT: P6, k3.

Row 8:
RIGHT FRONT: K6, k2tog, k1.
RIGHT SLEEVE: K1, k2tog, k18, k2tog, k1.
BACK: K1, k2tog, k12, k2tog, k1.
LEFT SLEEVE: K1, k2tog, k18, k2tog, k1.
LEFT FRONT: K1, k2tog, k6.

Row 9:
LEFT FRONT: K3, p5.
LEFT SLEEVE: P22.
BACK: P16.
RIGHT SLEEVE: P22.
RIGHT FRONT: P5, k3.

Row 10:
RIGHT FRONT: K5, k2tog, k1.
RIGHT SLEEVE: K1, k2tog, k16, k2tog, k1.
BACK: K1, k2tog, k10, k2tog, k1.
LEFT SLEEVE: K1, k2tog, k16, k2tog, k1.
LEFT FRONT: K1, k2tog, k5.

Row 11:
LEFT FRONT: K3, p4.
LEFT SLEEVE: P20.
BACK: P14.
RIGHT SLEEVE: P20.
RIGHT FRONT: P4, k3.

Row 12:
RIGHT FRONT: K4, k2tog, k1.
RIGHT SLEEVE: K1, k2tog, k14, k2tog, k1.
BACK: K1, k2tog, k8, k2tog, k1.
LEFT SLEEVE: K1, k2tog, k14, k2tog, k1.
LEFT FRONT: K1, k2tog, k4.

Row 13:
LEFT FRONT: K3, p3.
LEFT SLEEVE: P18.
BACK: P12.
RIGHT SLEEVE: P18.
RIGHT FRONT: P3, k3.

Row 14:
RIGHT FRONT: K3, k2tog, k1.
RIGHT SLEEVE: K1, k2tog, k12, k2tog, k1.
BACK: K1, k2tog, k6, k2tog, k1.
LEFT SLEEVE: K1, k2tog, k12, k2tog, k1.
LEFT FRONT: K1, k2tog, k3.

Row 15:
LEFT FRONT: K3, p2.
LEFT SLEEVE: P16.
BACK: P10.
RIGHT SLEEVE: P16.
RIGHT FRONT: P2, k3.

Row 16:
RIGHT FRONT: K5.
RIGHT SLEEVE: K1, k2tog, k10, k2tog, k1.
BACK: K1, k2tog, k4, k2tog, k1.
LEFT SLEEVE: K1, k2tog, k10, k2tog, k1.
LEFT FRONT: K5.

Row 17:
LEFT FRONT: K3, p2.
LEFT SLEEVE: P14.
BACK: P8.
RIGHT SLEEVE: P14.
RIGHT FRONT: P2, k3.

Row 18:
RIGHT FRONT: K5.
RIGHT SLEEVE: K1, k2tog, k8, k2tog, k1.
BACK: K1, k2tog, k2, k2tog, k1.
LEFT SLEEVE: K1, k2tog, k8, k2tog, k1.
LEFT FRONT: K5.

Row 19:
LEFT FRONT: K3, p2.
LEFT SLEEVE: P12.
BACK: P6.
RIGHT SLEEVE: P12.
RIGHT FRONT: P2, k3.

Row 20:
RIGHT FRONT: K5.
RIGHT SLEEVE: K1, k2tog, k6, k2tog, k1.
BACK: K1, k2tog, k2tog, k1.
LEFT SLEEVE: K1, k2tog, k6, k2tog, k1.
LEFT FRONT: K5.

Row 21:
LEFT FRONT: K3, p2.
LEFT SLEEVE: P10.
BACK: P4.
RIGHT SLEEVE: P10.
RIGHT FRONT: P2, k3.

Row 22:
RIGHT FRONT: K5.
RIGHT SLEEVE: K1, k2tog, k4, k2tog, k1.
BACK: K4.
LEFT SLEEVE: K1, k2tog, k4, k2tog, k1.
LEFT FRONT: K5.

Now work raglan shaping only on sleeves and back until 30 sts total remain. Work the last shaping row only on the sleeves.

Change to smaller needles and work 5 rows k2, p2 rib. BO in rib.

With crochet hook, sc along the edge sts of the bands, making chains as needed for button loops.

Weave in all ends on WS. Carefully steam press garment and then sew on buttons.

Here's a pattern for a dress with straps fastened with 2 buttons at the front. The dress can be worn over a thin sweater. The chart shows the pattern for the stitches on one needle, so you have to work the charted stitches 4 times total.

MATERIALS

1 set of 5 dpn U.S. sizes 1.5 and 2.5 (2.5 and 3 mm)
Crochet hook U.S. size C or D (3 mm)
Yarn appropriate for needles, such as Daletta, Babyull or Falk
2 buttons ⅜ in (1 cm) diameter

With smaller needles, CO 96 sts and divide evenly over 4 dpn = 24 sts on each needle. Join, being careful not to twist cast-on row.

Work garter stitch edging for hem:
RND 1: Purl.
RND 2: Knit.
RND 3: Purl.
RND 4: Knit.
RND 5: Purl.
RNDS 6-10: Change to larger needles and k96.

RND 11: *K1, k2tog, k18, k2tog, k1*; rep from * to * around.
RNDS 12-15: K88.
RND 16: *K1, k2tog, k16, k2tog, k1*; rep from * to * around.
RNDS 17-20: K80.
RND 21: *K1, k2tog, k14, k2tog, k1*; rep from * to * around.
RNDS 22-25: K72.
RND 26: *K1, k2tog, k12, k2tog, k1*; rep from * to * around.
RNDS 27-30: K64.
RND 31: *K1, k2tog, k10, k2tog, k1*; rep from * to * around.
RNDS 32-35: K56.
RND 36: *K1, k2tog, k8, k2tog, k1*; rep from * to * around.
RNDS 37-40: K48.
RND 41: *K1, k2tog, k6, k2tog, k1*; rep from * to * around.
RNDS 42-45: K40.

RND 46: *K1, k2tog, k4, k2tog, k1*; rep from * to * around.
RNDS 47: K32.
RND 48: K2, BO 4, k12 (including last st from bind-off), BO 4, k10 (including last st from bind-off), + the first 2 sts on ndl 1 = k12.
Going back over the sts of the last row, set aside the sts on each side of the armhole shaping on separate needles = 12 sts on each needle. Now work the back and front separately.

BACK
Row 1 (WS): Purl.
Row 2: Knit.
Row 3: Purl.
Row 4: Knit.
Row 5: Purl.
Row 6: Knit.
Row 7: P4, BO 4 purlwise, p4 (including the last st from bind-off). Now make 2 straps separately with 4 sts each: Work 7 rows back and forth, beginning on RS. BO purlwise.

FRONT
Row 1 (RS): Knit.
Row 2: Purl.
Row 3: Knit.
Row 4: Purl.
Row 5: Knit.
Row 6: Purl
BO knitwise.

Edge the yoke with single crochet and then crochet loops at the end of each strap for the buttonholes: Ch 4, sc in first corner and then work 5 sc back across loop.
Weave in all ends on WS. Steam press dress.
Sew buttons on top of front to match button loops on straps.

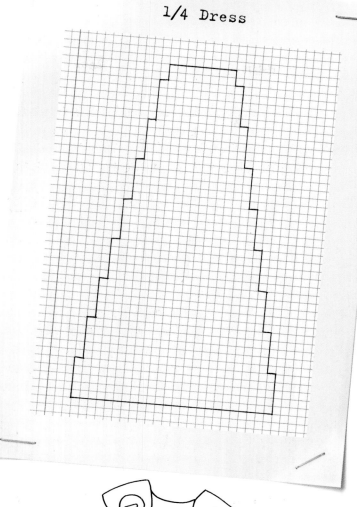

1/4 Dress

This dress is basically the same as the one in Basic Pattern 10. The only difference is that this one has short sleeves and you can close the top at the back with 2 small buttons.

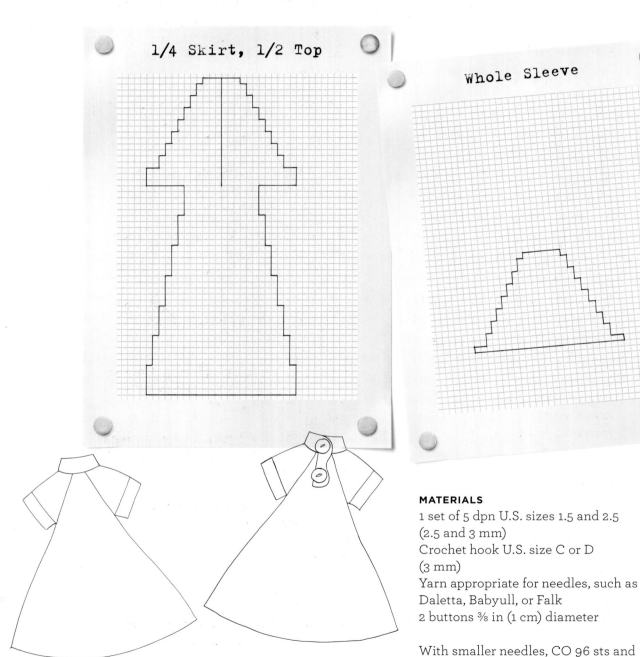

1/4 Skirt, 1/2 Top

Whole Sleeve

MATERIALS

1 set of 5 dpn U.S. sizes 1.5 and 2.5 (2.5 and 3 mm)
Crochet hook U.S. size C or D (3 mm)
Yarn appropriate for needles, such as Daletta, Babyull, or Falk
2 buttons ⅜ in (1 cm) diameter

With smaller needles, CO 96 sts and divide evenly over 4 dpn = 24 sts on each needle. Join, being careful not to twist cast-on row.

WORK GARTER STITCH EDGING FOR HEM:
RND 1: Purl.
RND 2: Knit.
RND 3: Purl.
RND 4: Knit.
RND 5: Purl.
RNDS 6-10: Change to larger needles and k96.
RND 11: *K1, k2tog, k18, k2tog, k1*; rep from * to * around.
RNDS 12-15: K88.
RND 16: *K1, k2tog, k16, k2tog, k1*; rep from * to * around.
RNDS 17-20: K80.
RND 21: *K1, k2tog, k14, k2tog, k1*; rep from * to * around.
RNDS 22-25: K72.
RND 26: *K1, k2tog, k12, k2tog, k1*; rep from * to * around.
RNDS 27-30: K64.
RND 31: *K1, k2tog, k10, k2tog, k1*; rep from * to * around.
RNDS 32-35: K56.
RND 36: *K1, k2tog, k8, k2tog, k1*; rep from * to * around.
RNDS 37-40: K48.
RND 41: K6 from ndl 1; turn and p48. Now work back and forth.
Row 42: K48.
Row 43: P48.
Row 44: K10, BO 4, k20 (including last st from bind-off), BO 4, k10 (including last st from bind-off).

SLEEVES
With smaller needles, CO 24 sts and divide evenly over 4 dpn. Join and work garter st in the round:
RND 1: Purl.
RND 2: Knit.
RND 3: Purl.
RND 4: Knit.
RND 5: Purl.

Change to larger needles.
RND 1: Knit.
RND 2: BO 2, k22 (including last st from bind-off), BO the last 2 sts.

Place the sleeve sts on one dpn and work the other sleeve the same way.

JOIN SLEEVES AND BODY
Begin at back opening:
Row 1: K10 for left back, k20 for left sleeve, k20 for front, k20 for right sleeve, k10 for right back. Turn and purl back.
Row 2: P7, *p2tog, p2, p2tog, p14*; repeat from * to * until 13 sts remain and end with p2tog, p2, p2tog, p7.
Row 3: K72.
Row 4: P6, *p2tog, p2, p2tog, p12*; repeat from * to * until 12 sts remain and end with p2tog, p2, p2tog, p6.
Row 5: K64.
Row 6: P5, *p2tog, p2, p2tog, p10*; repeat from * to * until 11 sts remain and end with p2tog, p2, p2tog, p5.
Row 7: K56.
Row 8: P4, *p2tog, p2, p2tog, p8*; repeat from * to * until 10 sts remain and end with p2tog, p2, p2tog, p4.
Row 9: K48.
Row 10: P3, *p2tog, p2, p2tog, p6*; repeat from * to * until 9 sts remain and end with p2tog, p2, p2tog, p3.
Row 11: K40.
Row 12: P2, *p2tog, p2, p2tog, p4*; repeat from * to * until 8 sts remain and end with p2tog, p2, p2tog, p2.
Row 13: K32.
Row 14: P1, *p2tog, p2, p2tog, p2*; repeat from * to * until 7 sts remain and end with p2tog, p2, p2tog, p1.

Change to smaller needles and knit 5 rows garter stitch.
Row 1: Purl.
Row 2: Knit.
Row 3: Purl.
Row 4: Knit.
Row 5: Purl.
BO. Edge neck opening with single crochet and make 2 button loops on band at back.
Weave in all ends on WS and carefully steam press dress. Sew on buttons across from loops on back.

We used Daletta to knit both the black dress that Lolita is wearing in Chapter 11 and the white nightgown that Sissel wears in Chapter 16. This basic design can be adapted for many outfits, such as a pink princess dress or a white dress for a Christmas angel if you add a pair of wings on the back.

MATERIALS
1 set of 5 dpn U.S. sizes 1.5 and 2.5 (2.5 and 3 mm); short circular U.S. size 2.5 (3 mm). Yarn: Daletta Natural 0020 **(this pattern needs 2 balls)**

WITH SHORT CIRCULAR U.S. 2.5 (3 MM), CO 100 STS; JOIN, BEING CAREFUL NOT TO TWIST CAST-ON STS.

RND 1: Purl.

RND 2: K1tbl, yo, k3, sl 1, k2tog, psso, k3, yo*; rep from * to * around.

RND 3: Knit.

RND 4: *K2, yo, k2, sl 1, k2tog, psso, k2, yo, k1*; rep from * to * around.

RND 5: Knit.

RND 6: K1 and place a marker for side between this st and the next, *yo, k2, yo, k1, sl 1, k2tog, psso, k1, yo, k1, k2tog*; rep from * to * around.

RND 7: Knit.

RND 8: *K2, k2tog, yo, sl 1, k2tog, psso, yo, sl 1, k1, psso, k1*; rep from * to * around.

RND 9: Knit.

RND 10: *K1, k2tog, yo, k1tbl, yo, k1tbl, yo, k1tbl, yo, sl 1, k1, psso*; rep from * to * around.
Move side marker forward to the last yarnover.

RND 11: Knit.

RND 12: *Sl 1, k2tog, psso, yo, k7, yo*; rep from * to * around.

RND 13: Knit.

Repeat Rnds 2-13 6 times and then work Rnds 2-9 once more.

RND 94: *K1, k2tog, k3, sl 1, k1, psso*; rep from * to * around.

RND 95: Knit.

Now divide sts onto 4 dpn = 15 sts on each needle.
Knit 5 rnds.

RND 101: *K1, k2tog, k9, k2tog, k1*; rep from * to * around.
Knit 5 rnds.

RND 107: *K1, k2tog, k7, k2tog, k1*; rep from * to * around.
Knit 5 rnds.

RND 113: *K1, k2tog, k5, k2tog, k1*; rep from * to * around.
Knit 5 rnds.

RND 119: *K1, k2tog, k3, k2tog, k1*; rep from * to * around.

RND 120: BO 2, k10 (including last st from bind-off), BO 4, k10 (including last st from bind-off), BO 2.
Place the 10 sts each for front and back onto separate needles.

SLEEVES

With smaller needles, CO 24 sts and divide over 4 dpn = 6 sts on each needle. Join.

RND 1: Purl.

RND 2: Knit.

RND 3: Purl.

RND 4: Change to larger needles and knit.

RNDS 5-33: Knit.

RND 34: BO 2, k20 (including last st from bind-off). BO last 2 sts.

Place sts onto one dpn and make the other sleeve the same way.

Join Sleeves and Body:

RND 121: K10 for back, k20 for left sleeve, k10 for front, k20 for right sleeve.

RND 122: Knit, shaping sleeves at the same time: k1, k2tog, k14, k2tog, k1.

RND 123: Knit.

RND 124: Knit, shaping sleeves at the same time: k1, k2tog, k12, k2tog, k1.

RND 125: Knit.

RND 126: Knit, shaping sleeves at the same time: k1, k2tog, k10, k2tog, k1.

RND 127: Knit.

RND 128: Knit, shaping sleeves at the same time: k1, k2tog, k8, k2tog, k1.

RND 129: Knit.

RND 130: Knit, shaping sleeves at the same time: k1, k2tog, k6, k2tog, k1.

Change to smaller needles and work 15 rounds k2, p2 rib.
BO. Sew underarm seams. Weave in all ends on WS.
Carefully steam press dress.

NOTE Do not press the ribbing at the neck.

This cute little sweater can be worn over a dress or paired with pants. A must-have garment for every stylish doll's wardrobe.

MATERIALS

1 set of 5 dpn U.S. sizes 1.5 and 2.5 (2.5 and 3 mm); two 12 in (30 cm) straight needles U.S. size 2.5 (3 mm)
Yarn: Falk or Daletta recommended for this sweater
4 small buttons

BODY (including garter stitch band with buttonholes)

With smaller needles, CO 52 sts.
Rows 1-3: Working back and forth, k52.
Row 4: K49, yo, k2tog, k1.
Rows 5-7: K52, working back and forth.
Row 8 Change to larger needles and k5, p42, k5.
Row 9: K52.
Row 10: K5, p42, k5.
Row 11: Knit.
Row 12: K5, p42, k2, yo, k2tog, k1.
Row 13: K52.
Row 14: K5, p42, k5.
Row 15: K52.
Row 16: K5, p42, k5.
Row 17: K12, BO 4, k20 (including last st from bind-off), BO 4, k12 (including last st from bind-off).

SLEEVES

With smaller needles, CO 24 sts and divide evenly onto 4 dpn = 6 sts on each needle. Join and work garter st in the round.

Rnd 1: Purl.
Rnd 2: Knit.
Rnd 3: Purl.
Rnd 4: Knit.
Rnd 5: Purl.

Change to larger needles and knit 24 rnds (1 ½ in / 4 cm). BO 2, k20 (including last st from bind-off), BO 2.

JOIN BODY AND SLEEVES

Row 18: Place sleeves and body onto one needle U.S. size 2.5 (3 mm). Place a marker between each sleeve and body (see drawing, p. 61).

Begin on WS: K5, p7 for front, p20 for sleeve, p20 for back, p20 for sleeve, p7 and k5 for front.
Begin raglan shaping:

Row 19: K12 for front, (k1, k2tog, k14, k2tog, k1) for sleeve, (k1, k2tog, k14, k2tog, k1) for back, (k1, k2tog, k14, k2tog, k1) for sleeve, k12 for front.
Row 20: K5, purl until 5 sts remain and end with k2, yo, k2tog, k1.
Row 21: K9, k2tog, k2, k2tog, k12, k2tog, k2, k2tog, k12, k2tog, k2, k2tog, k12, k2tog, k2, k2tog, k9.
Row 22: K5, purl until 5 sts remain and end k5.
Row 23: K8 (*k2tog, k2, k2tog, k10*; rep from * to * until 14 sts remain and end k2tog, k2, k2tog, k8.
Row 24: K5, purl until 5 sts remain and end k5.
Row 25: K7, *k2tog, k2, k2tog, k8*; rep from * to * until 13 sts remain and end k2tog, k2, k2tog, k7.
Row 26: K5, purl until 5 sts remain and end k5.
Row 27: K6, *k2tog, k2, k2tog, k6*; rep from * to * across.
Row 28: K5, purl until 5 sts remain and end with k2, yo, k2tog, k1.
Row 29: K5, *k2tog, k2, k2tog, k4*; rep from * to * until 11 sts remain and end k2tog, k2, k2tog, k5.
Row 30: Knit.
Row 31: K4, *k2tog, k2, k2tog, k2*; rep form * to * until 10 sts remain and end k2tog, k2, k2tog, k4.
Row 32: Knit.
Row 33: K7, *k2tog, k2tog, k2*; rep from * to * until 11 sts remain and end k2tog, k2tog, k7.
Row 34: Knit.
BO. Weave in all ends on WS. Carefully steam press sweater and then sew on buttons spaced as for buttonholes.

NOTE See Page 62 for tips on joining the body and sleeves.

Here's a jacket for cold winter days. If you add more repeats, it will be a lovely coat.

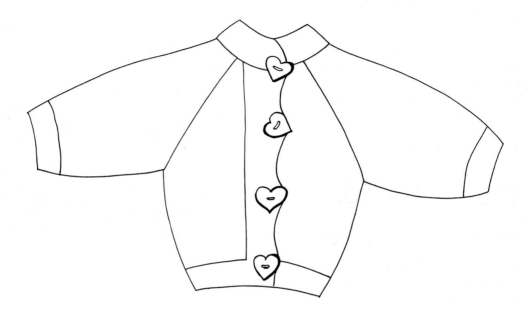

MATERIALS

1 set of 5 dpn U.S. sizes 1.5 and 2.5 (2.5 and 3 mm); 12 in (30 cm) straight needles U.S. size 2.5 (3 mm)
Crochet hook: U.S. size C or D (3 mm)
Yarn: Our sample is knit with Falk but this sweater can be knit with other types of yarn for the same needle sizes
4 small buttons

SLEEVES

With smaller needles, CO 24 sts and divide onto 4 dpn = 6 sts on each needle. Join, being careful not to twist cast-on row.
Work 5 rnds k2, p2 rib.

Change to larger needles and work an increase rnd: *k3, inc 1*; repeat from * to * around.
Increase for the last st on each needle through the side of the first st on the next needle.

Knit 20 rnds or desired sleeve length to underarm.
RND 21: BO the first 3 and last 3 sts of rnd. Place sleeve sts onto one needle = 26 sts.
Make the other sleeve the same way.

BODY

With smaller needles, CO 48 sts. Work back and forth with 5 rows k2, p2 rib. Change to larger needles and an increase row:
K6, inc 1, *k3, inc 1*; rep from * to * until 6 sts remain and end k6.
Continue working back and forth in stockinette (knit on RS and purl on WS).

NOTE Now begin and end each row with k3 for the button/buttonhole bands. Work back and forth in stockinette (knit on RS and purl on WS) with garter st bands until body measures 4 ¼ in (11 cm) long or desired length.

Shape armholes on RS: K12, BO 6, k25 (including last st from bind-off), BO 6, k12 (including last st from bind-off). Changing to straight needles and adding sleeves at sides, work next WS row.

Place markers at each intersection between the body and sleeves = 4 markers (see page 61).
Continue working back and forth, shaping raglan seam on RS rows by decreasing as follows on each side of markers: k2tog, k1, slip marker, k1, k2tog.

Decrease for raglan on every RS row until 45 sts remain. Work 1 WS row, increasing with M1 at center back, and then work 5 rows k2, p2 rib with smaller needles. With crochet hook, work 1 sc into last st on left front band.
On the right band, crochet the button loops and edging as follows:
4 sc, *ch 3 and 1 sc in every 3rd st from the chain. Turn and work 4 sc in each chain loop and then work 7 sc across top of band.

Finish with 2 sc, cut yarn. Seam underarms, weave in ends on WS. Carefully steam press jacket and then sew on buttons spaced as for button loops.

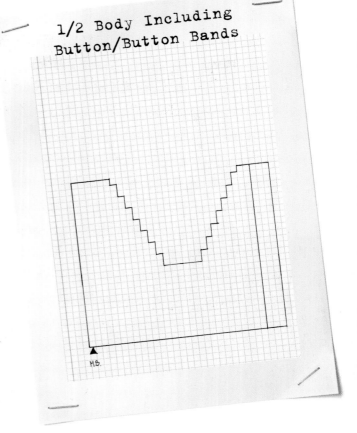

1/2 Body Including Button/Button Bands

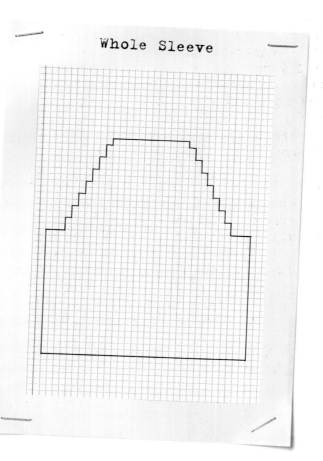

Whole Sleeve

A cape for the coolest doll out on a tour of the town.

MATERIALS

1 set of 5 dpn U.S. sizes 1.5 and 2.5
(2.5 and 3 mm)
Yarn appropriate for needle sizes above

We used a Norwegian crown coin (¾ in
(2 cm) in diameter) to measure the diameter of the pompoms. See Chapter 3 for
how to make pompoms.

With smaller needles, CO 64 sts and di-
vide evenly over 4 dpn = 16 sts on each
needle. Join, being careful not to twist
cast-on row.
Begin at the neck and work 30 rnds k2,
p2 rib.
Change to larger needles and work an
increase rnd: *K1, inc 1, k14, inc 1, k1*; rep
from * to * around.
Knit 20 rnds.
Finish the cape with a garter stitch edge
on smaller needles:
RND 1: Purl.
RND 2: Knit.
RND 3: Purl.
RND 4: Knit.
RND 5: Purl.
RND 6: Knit.
RND 7: Purl.
BO and weave in all ends on WS. Care-
fully steam press cape except for ribbing.
Make 13 pompoms and sew them evenly
spaced around the garter edging.

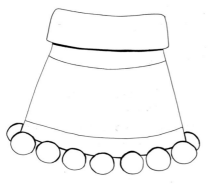

A simple alternative to a sweater, it's easy to knit and you can make lots of variations with embroidery.

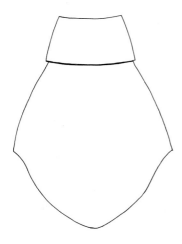

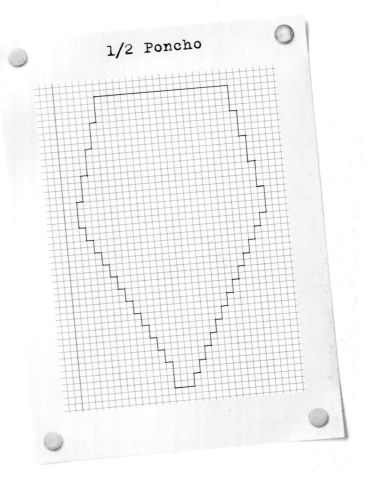

1/2 Poncho

MATERIALS
1 set of 5 dpn U.S. sizes 1.5 and 2.5 (2.5 and 3 mm)
Crochet hook U.S. size C or D (3 mm)
Yarn appropriate for needles

FIRST TRIANGLE
With larger needles, CO 3 sts.
Row 1: P3.
Row 2: K1, inc 1, k2.
Row 3: Purl 4.
Row 4: K1, inc 1, k2, inc 1, k1.
Row 5: P6.
Row 6: K1, inc 1, k4, inc 1, k1.
Row 7: P8.
Increase the same way on every RS row until there are a total of 28 sts.
Set aside first triangle and make the second triangle the same way.
Now divide the sts of each triangle onto 2 dpn = 14 sts on each needle for front and back. Join to work in the round.
RNDS 1-3: Knit.
RND 4: Shape sides: *K1, k2tog, k22, k2tog, k1*; rep from * to *.
RNDS 5-7: Knit.
RND 8: *K1, k2tog, k20, k2tog, k1*; rep from * to *.
RNDS 9-11. Knit.

RND 12: *K1, k2tog, k18, k2tog, k1*; rep from * to *.
RNDS 13-15: Knit.
RND 16: *K1, k2tog, k16, k2tog, k1*; rep from * to *.
RNDS 17-19: Knit.

Change to smaller needles and work 30 rnds k2, p2 rib. BO in rib.
With crochet hook, work sc around lower edge with 2 sc in each edge st.

Weave in ends on WS. Carefully steam press poncho except for ribbing.

Because most of the dolls have thick hair, hats aren't the easiest things for them to wear. For that reason, we only included two hats in the book.

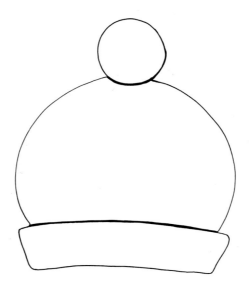

MATERIALS

1 set of 5 dpn U.S. sizes 7 and 8
(4.5 and 5 mm)
Yarn: Freestyle

With smaller needles, CO 36 sts and divide evenly over 4 dpn = 9 sts on each needle. Join, being careful not to twist cast-on row.
Work 15 rnds k2, p2 rib.
Change to larger needles.
Work an increase rnd: *K3, inc 1*; rep from * to * around.
RNDS 1-10: Knit.
RND 11: *K1, k2tog, k6, k2tog, k1*; rep from * to * around.
RND 12: Knit.

RND 13: *K1, k2tog, k4, k2tog, k1*; rep from * to * around.
RND 14: Knit.
RND 15: *K1, k2tog, k2, k2tog, k1*; rep from * to * around.
RND 16: Knit.
RND 17: *K1, k2tog, k2tog, k1*; rep from * to * around.
RND 18: Knit.
RND 19: *K1, k2tog, k1*; rep from * to * around.
Cut yarn and pull end through remaining 12 sts. Tighten and weave in end on WS.

Make a pompom and sew it to the top of the hat.

If you knit stripes, you can make many different hats from this one pattern.

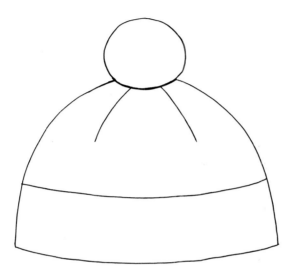

MATERIALS
1 set of 5 dpn U.S. sizes 1.5 and 2.5
(2.5 and 3 mm)
Yarn: Babyull:
Yellow
Red

With smaller needles, CO 64 sts and divide evenly over 4 dpn = 16 sts on each needle. Join, being careful not to twist cast-on row.
Work 15 rnds k2, p2 rib in the following color sequence: 5 rnds yellow, 5 rnds red, 5 rnds yellow.
Change to larger needles and, with red, knit 15 rnds.
RND 16: *K1, k2tog, k10, k2tog, k1*; rep from * to * around.
RND 17: K56.
RND 18: *K1, k2tog, k8, k2tog, k1*; rep from * to * around.
RND 19: K48.

RND 20: *K1, k2tog, k6, k2tog, k1*; rep from * to * around.
RND 21: K40.
RND 22: *K1, k2tog, k4, k2tog, k1*; rep from * to * around.
RND 23: K32.
RND 24: *K1, k2tog, k2, k2tog, k1*; rep from * to * around.
RND 25: K24.
RND 26: *K1, k2tog, k2tog, k1*; rep from * to * around.
RND 27: K16.
RND 28: *K1, k2tog, k1*; rep from * to * around.
Cut yarn and pull end through remaining 12 sts. Tighten and weave in end on WS. Carefully steam press hat except for ribbing.

Make a pompom and sew it to the top of the hat.

Here's the easiest solution for a head covering for a doll with a lot of hair.

HEADBAND

With U.S. size 2.5 (3 mm) needles and Falk, CO 20 sts. Knit back and forth in garter st until piece is 8 in (20 cm) long. BO. Seam short ends of band and weave in ends on WS. Double the band over the doll's head.

BASIC PATTERN 21: MITTENS

MATERIALS

1 set of 5 dpn U.S. sizes 1.5 and 2.5 (2.5 and 3 mm)
Yarn: Falk, Daletta, Hubro or similar yarn

With larger needles, CO 12 sts and divide evenly over 4 dpn = 3 sts on each needle. Join, being careful not to twist cast-on row.

Rnd 1: K12.
Rnd 2: *K1, inc 1, k4, inc 1, k1*; rep from * to * around.
Rnd 3: K16.
Rnd 4: *K1, inc 1, k6, inc 1, k1*; rep from * to * around.
Rnd 5: K20.
Rnd 6: *K1, inc 1, k8, inc 1, k1*; rep from * to * around.
Rnd 7: K24.
Rnd 8: *K1, inc 1, k10, inc 1, k1*; rep from * to * around.
Knit 18 rnds, approx 1 ¼ in (3 cm). Change to smaller needles and work 10 rnds k2, p2 rib.
BO. Reinforce top and then weave in ends on WS.

BASIC PATTERN 20: SCARF

MATERIALS

The scarves in the book are knitted with leftover yarn or Falk and Babyull. Straight needles U.S. size 2.5 (3 mm)

CO 22 sts.
Work in k2, p2 rib until scarf is desired length, approximately 11 ¾ in (30 cm).

MATERIALS

1 set of 5 dpn U.S. size 2.5 (3 mm)
Yarn appropriate for needles

CO 12 sts and divide evenly over 4 dpn = 3 sts on each needle. Join, being careful not to twist cast-on row.

RND 1: Knit.
RND 2: *K1, inc 1, k1, inc 1, k1*; rep from * to * around.
RND 3: Knit.
RND 4: *K1, inc 1, k3, inc 1, k1*; rep from * to * around.
RND 5: Knit.
RND 6: *K1, inc 1, k5, inc 1, k1*; rep from * to * around.
RND 7: Knit.
RND 8: Needles 1 and 2: P2, *k2, p2*; rep from * to * on needles 1 and 2.
NEEDLES 3 AND 4: Knit.
Repeat Rnd 8 10 more times.

HEEL

The heel is worked over the sts on needles 3 and 4.
Next rnd:
NDLS 1 AND 2: K2, p2 rib.
NDL 3: Knit.
NDL 4: K2, k2tog; turn.
NEXT ROW (WS): Sl 1, p5, p2tog; turn.
NEXT ROW (RS): Sl 1, k5, k2tog; turn.
Repeat the last 2 rows until all the stitches on ndls 3 and 4 have been worked (= 6 heel sts).
LAST HEEL ROW (RS): Sl 1, k5.
Now you are back at the original beginning of the rnd.
Continue working around in rib as follows:
NEXT RND: *P2, k2*; rep from * to * to end of rnd (= 24 sts).
Rep the last rnd for 25 rnds or until the leg is desired length.
BO in ribbing.
You can make sock or stockings, depending on the length.

What every doll wants is a pair of new shoes!

MATERIALS

1 set of 5 dpn U.S.size 7 (4.5 mm)
Yarn: Freestyle

CO 20 sts
Working back and forth, knit 7 rows.
Row 8: K1, k2tog, k14, k2tog, k1.
Rows 9-10: Knit.
Row 11: K1, k2tog, k12, k2tog, k1.
Rows 12-13: Knit.
Row 14: K1, k2tog, k10, k2tog, k1.
Rows 15-16: Knit.
Row 17: K1, k2tog, k8, k2tog, k1.
Row 18: K1, k2tog, k6, k2tog, k1.
Row 19: K1, k2tog, k4, k2tog, k1.
BO. Seam front and heel.

All the shoes are knit with Freestyle on needles U.S. size 7 (4.5 mm).

Decorate the shoes with BUTTONS, pompoms, embroidery, or crocheted flowers.

One of our most important sources of inspiration has always been traditional knitting motifs and vintage sweaters. It's completely natural that we begin this section of the book by sending the dolls off into the mountains so they can show off their lovely sweaters and enjoy themselves skiing and *eating oranges.*

OUTFIT 1

A sweater inspired by an old postcard from Finland that we found in the archives of the Norwegian Institute for National Costumes and Folk Clothing in Fagernes. The shoes are knitted with Freestyle cornflower blue 5626 and the glasses are made with fine steel wire wrapped with black yarn to shape the frames.

1/2 Body

Whole Sleeve

1. MULTICOLORED SWEATER
BASIC PATTERN 2, PAGE 60.
MATERIALS: Dale of Norway Falk:
Black 0090, Bluebell 5624,
Off white 0017, Red 4018, Dandelion 2417

2. BEIGE KNICKERBOCKERS
BASIC PATTERN 8, PAGE 72
MATERIALS: Dale of Norway,
Sandlewood 2642

CARLOS AND CARLOS wearing matching sweaters. It is fun to work with the design process in miniature before we make the adult sizes!

OUTFIT 2

Arne in a classic ski ensemble.
With red knickerbockers and a
Setesdal sweater he is ready for
the mountains and plateaus.

Whole Sleeve

1/2 Body

3. SETESDAL PATTERN SWEATER
BASIC PATTERN 2, PAGE 60.
MATERIALS Dale of Norway Falk:
Burgundy 4227
Natural 0020

4. RED KNICKERBOCKERS
BASIC PATTERN 8, PAGE 72
MATERIALS Dale of Norway Falk:
Red 4018

Outfit 3

Everyone knows that you should dress in red on the ski trails in the mountains to be visible. This doll has certainly done that.

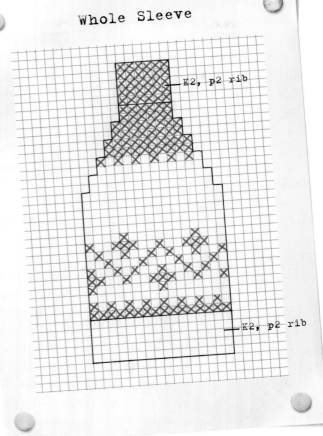

Whole Sleeve

K2, p2 rib

K2, p2 rib

Vivian

10. THICK SWEATER WITH COLOR MOTIFS
Basic Pattern 4, page 66
MATERIALS Dale of Norway Freestyle:
Off white 0020, Red 4018

11. RED PANTS
Basic Pattern 7A, page 69
MATERIALS Dale of Norway Falk:
Burgundy 4227

12. HAT WITH POMPOM
Basic Pattern 18, page 89
MATERIALS Dale of Norway Daletta:
Red 4018
Yellow 2015

75. MITTENS
Basic Pattern 21, page 90
MATERIALS Dale of Norway Falk:
Off white 0017

SÖT SPORTJUMPER

FÖR UNGA FRÖKEN

SPORTY WOMEN: The sweater was inspired
by a Swedish pamphlet that we bought in a
second-hand shop in Göteborg. We took the
colors from a French drawing of the 1920's.

1/2 Body

OUTFIT 4

This sweater was inspired by a Swedish sports sweater for young women. Our version is also similar to an Icelander sweater.

Vivian

75. PURPLE MITTENS
BASIC PATTERN 21, PAGE 90
MATERIALS Dale of Norway Falk:
Iris purple 5144

5. ICELANDER
BASIC PATTERN 2, PAGE 60
MATERIALS Dale of Norway Falk:
Sand 2611
Green 8246
Red 4018
Dark turquoise 6215

6. GREEN PANTS
BASIC PATTERN 7A, PAGE 69
MATERIALS Dale of Norway Falk:
Fern 9155

THE LEGS FOR THE PANTS ARE 5 ¼ IN (13 CM) LONG BEFORE THE BIND-OFF.

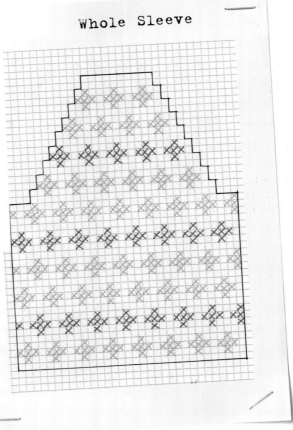

Whole Sleeve

OUTFIT 5

Arne is ready to enjoy the sunshine in his hat, socks, and jacket. The jacket was inspired by a Dale of Norway booklet for the Ski championships in 1966.

Whole Sleeve

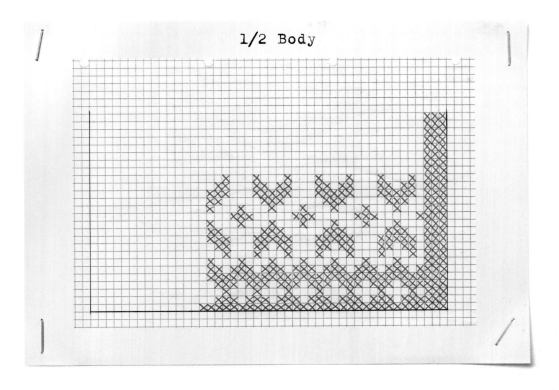

1/2 Body

7. JACKET INSPIRED BY A DALE OF NORWAY SWEATER FOR THE SKI CHAMPIONSHIPS IN 1966
BASIC PATTERN 14, PAGE 84
MATERIALS Dale of Norway Falk:
Bottle-green 7053 (pattern color)
Natural 0020

Make an extra little ball of yarn and knit one of the front bands with it. Twist the natural and bottle-green yarns around each other when changing colors.

5 rnds: Work the ribbing on the body and sleeves in the main color, Bottle-green 7053. The first row on the chart is the round with increases.
Work on the body until it is 3 ¼ in (8 cm) long and then shape the armholes. Work the last row before the neck ribbing with the main color.

4. RED KNICKERBOCKERS
BASIC PATTERN 8, PAGE 72
MATERIALS Dale of Norway Falk:
Red 4018

8. HAT WITH POMPOM
BASIC PATTERN 17, PAGE 88
MATERIALS Dale of Norway Freestyle:
Blue 6135
Off white for pompom 0020

9. SOCKS
BASIC PATTERN 22, PAGE 91
MATERIALS Dale of Norway Falk:
Sea green 6943

THE NUMBER 1 RULE FOR THE DOLLS WHEN THEY
ARE IN THE MOUNTAINS: NEVER LOSE SIGHT OF
YOUR HOUSE WHEN OUT SKIING AND HIKING.

Agnethe

WE LOVE RED AND WHITE
GINGHAM AS WELL AS
KITCHEN TOWELS, KITCHEN
CURTAINS, AND BLUE AND
WHITE CHINA.

In this chapter, we've focused on making outfits that the dolls can wear either for coffee breaks at home or when going out for coffee in town. Everyone knows dolls drink a lot of coffee and tea, so let's set the table with our best miniature service and bring out the cakes and goodies!

OUTFIT 6

The basic jacket has been transformed into a sporty jeans jacket by embroidering orange lines with back stitch.

13. JEANS JACKET
BASIC PATTERN 14 PAGE 84
MATERIALS Dale of Norway Falk:
Norwegian blue 5744
Orange 3309

With orange 3309, embroider the lines for a jeans look with back stitch.

11. RED PANTS
BASIC PATTERN 7A, PAGE 69
MATERIALS Dale of Norway Falk:
Burgundy 4227

Beate

OUTFIT 7

"I am very concerned about war and peace and such topics and really love animals, especially rabbits, and might want to be a pop star or to be on TV."

Sissel 🌼

We found this rabbit motif on a pair of rompers in the Woman and Clothing Knitting Book published in 1948.

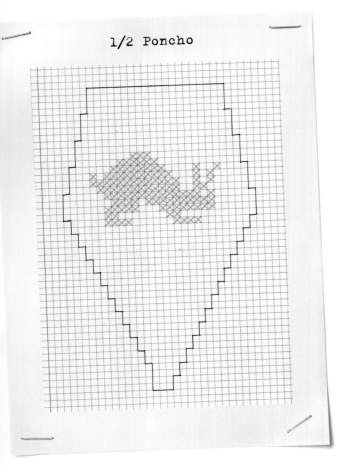

1/2 Poncho

14. PONCHO WITH RABBIT
BASIC PATTERN 16, PAGE 87
MATERIALS Dale of Norway Falk:
Natural 0020
Peony 4516

Finish the poncho by embroidering the rabbit with duplicate stitch (see page 26). Carefully steam press poncho.

15. HEADBAND WITH POMPOMS
BASIC PATTERN 19, PAGE 90
MATERIALS Dale of Norway Falk:
Natural 0020

We traced around a small coffee cup to measure the template for the pompoms. See page 26 for more on how to make pompoms.

ONCE YOU'VE KNIT ONE *doll it won't be long before you knit some more. Take a break and enjoy a cup of coffee with your new doll.*

COFFEE-BRITT, *put on the kettle,*
COFFEE-BRITT, *put on the kettle,*
COFFEE-BRITT, *put on the kettle,*
the guests are arriving now.

COFFEE-BRITT, *turn off the kettle,*
COFFEE-BRITT, *turn off the kettle,*
COFFEE-BRITT *turn off the kettle,*
for now the guests have gone.

"RHYMES AND RULES FOR EVERY CHILD"
Retold in Norwegian by Alf Prøysen and then into English by C. Rhoades

Outfit 8

A dress inspired by our favorite red and white gingham blocks. For this design, we drew hearts in the squares and arranged the breaks in the pattern as if dress were to be sewn. Brand new heart buttons fasten the dress at the shoulders. It's a great dress to wear in the kitchen or at a coffee break with friends.

Kaja

1/4 Dress

16. GINGHAM DRESS
BASIC PATTERN 10, PAGE 76
MATERIALS Dale of Norway Falk:
Red 4018
Natural 0020

OUTFIT 9

Stylish green cape and green ear warmer that contrast well with Siv's red hair.

Siv

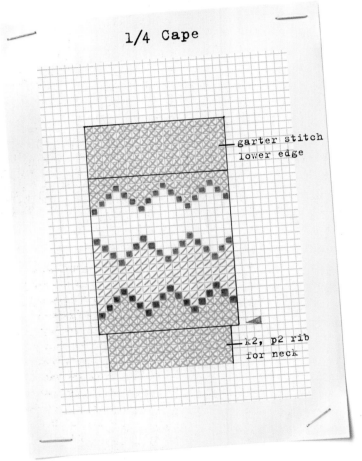

1/4 Cape

garter stitch lower edge

k2, p2 rib for neck

17. CAPE WITH POMPOMS
BASIC PATTERN 15, PAGE 86
MATERIALS Dale of Norway Falk:
Lime green 8817
Kelly green 8246
Pastel green 7502
Norwegian blue 5744

Cast on with Lime green 8817 and work the k2, p2 rib for the neck. The arrow indicates the increase row.

18. HEADBAND WITH POMPOMS (EAR WARMER)
With needles U.S. size 2.5 (3 mm), CO 8 sts. Work back and forth in garter stitch until piece is 9 ½ in (24 cm) long. BO and cut yarn, leaving tail long enough for sewing band together. Seam band and weave in ends on WS. Securely sew a pompom over each ear for the ear warmer. We traced around a Norwegian one crown coin (¾ in / 2 cm diameter) for the pompom template.

See Chapter 3, page 26 for how to make pompoms.

OUTFIT 10

1/2 Body, Whole Sleeve

Kaja

BY EMBROIDERING with duplicate stitch, you can make a lot of fun sweaters and the doll's wardrobe will grow quickly this way. We found the cat motif in the *Women and Clothing Knitting Book* published in 1948. We changed the cat a bit so the motif would look good in embroidery.

21. TOP WITH CAT
BASIC PATTERN 2, PAGE 60
MATERIALS Dale of Norway Falk:
Aquamarine 6604
Barn red 4137

Begin at the neck and then continue with needles U.S. 1.5 (2.5 mm), working an eyelet row: *K2tog, yo, p2*; rep from * to * around. Work 8 rnds k2, p2 rib for lower edge and then BO.
Seam the underarms and weave in ends on WS. Carefully steam press.
Crochet a chain stitch cord and thread through the hole row.

Embroider the cat with duplicate stitch (see page 26) and steam press garment again.

22. WHITE PANTS
BASIC PATTERN 7A, PAGE 69
MATERIALS Dale of Norway Falk: Off white 0017

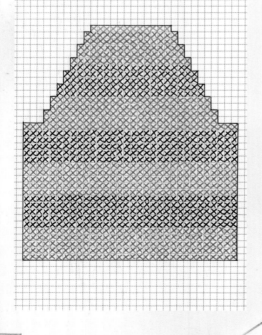

OUTFIT 11

The City Shorts and a stylish striped
top make a great combination for
checking out the shops in town.

Whole Sleeve

1/2 Body

Beate

19. SHORT SLEEVE TOP

Basic Pattern 2, page 60
MATERIALS Dale of Norway Falk:
Kelly green 8246
Ocean blue 6027
Black 0090

SLEEVES AND BODY

Cast on with needles U.S. size 1.5 (2.5 mm) and Green 8246. Begin garter stitch edging:
RND 1: Purl.
RND 2: Knit.
RND 3: Purl.
RND 4: Knit.
RND 5: Purl.
Change to U.S. 2.5 (3 mm) needles and continue, following the chart.

Work the raglan shaping until 14 sts remain on each half of the body and then work the last blue rnd on the chart. Change to smaller needles and green: *K1, k2tog, k8, k2tog, k1*; rep from * to *. Now work 10 rnds k2, p2 rib and bind off. Weave in ends on WS and carefully steam press sweater except for the ribbed neckband.

20. SHORTS

Basic Pattern 7A, page 69
MATERIALS
Dale of Norway Falk:
Sand heather 0004

Make the leg 1 ½ in (4 cm) long and then bind off.

76. HEADBAND

Basic Pattern 19, page 90
MATERIALS
Dale of Norway Falk:
Spring green 9133

"With this headband on, I don't need any black embroidered eyebrows."

SHOP • 136

Duggal
ly wears a jacket and skirt
zi,
rom Family Jewels, socks by Hue... Shoes are Dolly's own

PLAY WITH
ME

LARGE
PORTION

Chapter 10
SWEETS

We gathered up everything sweet that we could find in the house: old Dolly Parton collages, buttons in sweet and sour colors, candy canes, Big Ben, drops, sweetheart candies...*When they wear clothes with colors from the candy store the dolls look good enough to eat!*

You'll get some candy and chocolates,
You'll go to the movies and the café...
Hans Erichsen/Einar Kristoffersen

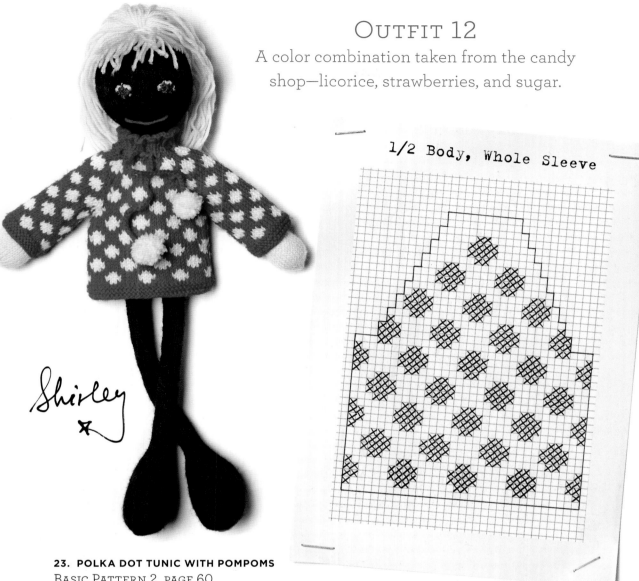

OUTFIT 12
A color combination taken from the candy shop—licorice, strawberries, and sugar.

1/2 Body, Whole Sleeve

Shirley ✗

23. POLKA DOT TUNIC WITH POMPOMS
BASIC PATTERN 2, PAGE 60
MATERIALS Dale of Norway Falk:
Red 4018
Off white 0017
Trace around a ¾ in (2 cm) coin for the pompom templates.

Begin the sleeves and body with a garter stitch edging:
RND 1: Purl.
RND 2: Knit.
RND 3: Purl.
RND 4: Knit.
RND 5: Purl.

Continue, following the chart up to the neck.

Begin neck, changing to needles U.S. 1.5 (2.5 mm):
Hole rnd: *K2tog, yo, p2*; rep from * to * around.
Work 8 rnds k2, p2 rib and then BO.

Seam underarms and weave in ends on WS. Carefully steam press tunic. Crochet a chain stitch cord and thread it through the hole rnd. Make 2 small pompoms and attach one to each end of the crochet cord.

75. MITTENS
BASIC PATTERN 21, PAGE 90
MATERIALS Dale of Norway Falk:
Off white 0017

Outfit 13

This girl looks like she just jumped out of a bag of Big Ben candies.

1/2 Body

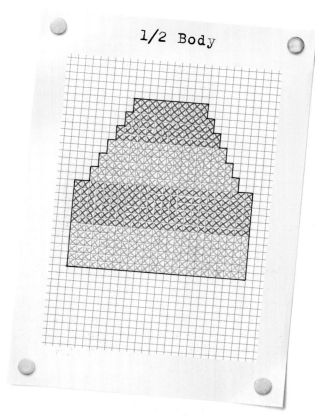

Maja

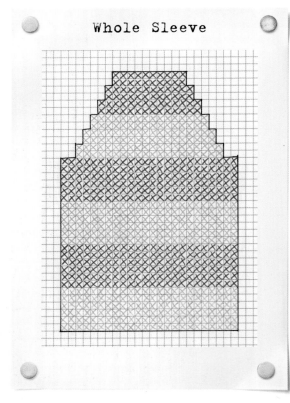

Whole Sleeve

24. STRIPED SWEATER
BASIC PATTERN 3, PAGE 64
MATERIALS Dale of Norway Babyull:
Navy 5755
Pastel pink 4711

25. BALLERINA SKIRT
BASIC PATTERN 6, PAGE 68
MATERIALS Dale of Norway Falk:
Blossom 4203
Off white 0017

75. MITTENS
BASIC PATTERN 21, PAGE 90
MATERIALS Dale of Norway Falk:
Pink 4510

OUTFIT 14

When she is wearing this skirt,
Siv just wants to twirl around
and around. The T-shirt is knitted
directly on the doll (see Chapter 6, p. 51,
for underwear instructions).

Siv

26. SKIRT WITH POLKA DOTS AND A RUFFLED EDGE
BASIC PATTERN 6, PAGE 68
MATERIALS Dale of Norway Daletta:
White 0010
Pastel pink 4711

The chart below includes the ribbed edging;
begin charted rows at the bottom with the first
round after the cast-on.

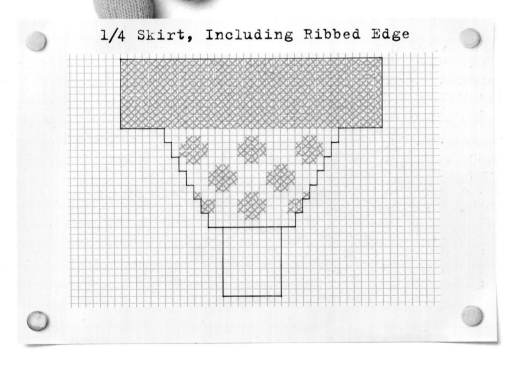

1/4 Skirt, Including Ribbed Edge

Outfit 15

The thin sweater fits perfectly under the overalls. The little flower buttons are old but you can find a big selection of flower buttons at the store.

Sissel 🌼

BACK OF the overalls

27. STRIPED SWEATER
Basic Pattern 3, page 64
MATERIALS Dale of Norway Babyull:
Natural 0020
Pink 4504
The ribbed edges are worked in pink.

28. OVERALLS
Basic Pattern 7B, page 71
MATERIALS Dale of Norway Falk:
Soft blue 5943
Peony 4516

1/2 Body

Whole Sleeve

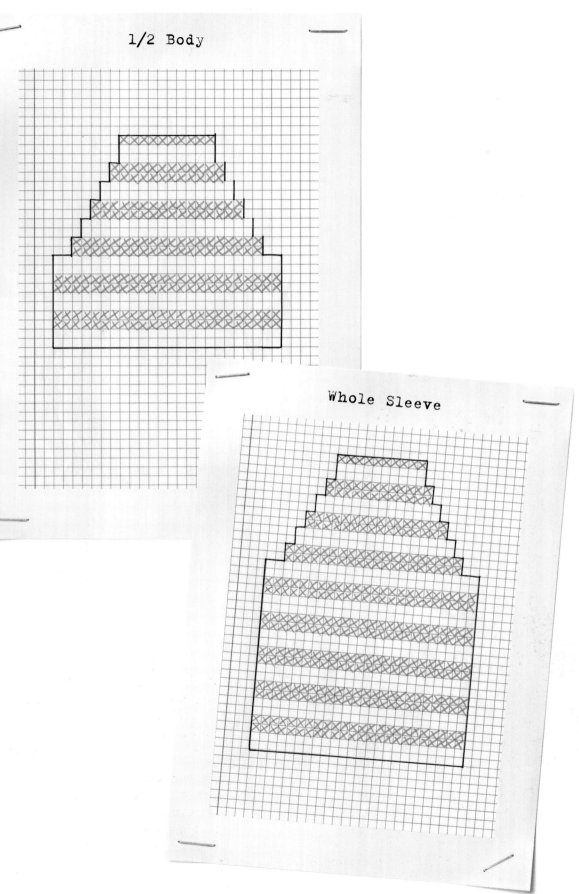

25¢

Taste Sample

"HERE WE ARE
at the counter in
our work clothes
that match the
goodies we sell."

OUTFIT 16

The thin sweater can be worn under dresses like this so you'll have lots of fun options to mix and match.

1/4 Dress

29. PURPLE SWEATER
BASIC PATTERN 3, PAGE 64

We knit this sweater with some leftover yarn. Babyull comes in three shades of purple: Lupine 5226, Pale iris 5302 or Purple 5245

30. GREEN DRESS WITH WHITE POLKA DOTS
BASIC PATTERN 10, PAGE 76
MATERIALS Dale of Norway Falk:
Lime green 8817
Off white 0017

75. MITTENS
BASIC PATTERN 21, PAGE 90
MATERIALS Dale of Norway Falk:
Off white 0017

OUTFIT 17
This girl has never been afraid of colors.

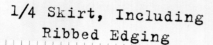

1/4 Skirt, Including Ribbed Edging

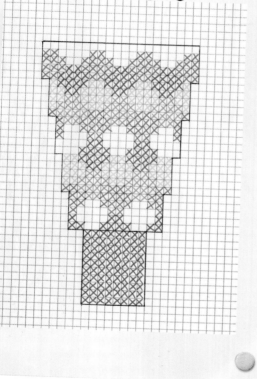

31. YELLOW SWEATER
BASIC PATTERN 3, PAGE 64
MATERIALS Dale of Norway Babyull:
Pastel yellow 2203

32. MULTICOLOR POLKA DOTTED SKIRT
BASIC PATTERN 5, PAGE 67
MATERIALS Dale of Norway Babyull:
White 0010
Fuchsia pink 4516
Tangerine 2817
Sunny yellow 2106
Lagoon 6435

Knit the last round on the chart with U.S. size 1.5 (2.5 mm) needles and then bind off.
Crochet the edging: Work 1 sc in the last bound-off stitch, *ch 4, 1 sc in the 3rd edge st from the chain loop*; rep from * to * around. On the next round, work 5 sc in each chain loop; end with 1 sl st to first sc. Weave in ends on WS and carefully steam press outfit.

33. STRIPED SCARF
BASIC PATTERN 20, PAGE 90
MATERIALS Dale of Norway Babyull:
Tangerine 2817
Mushroom 2621

With U.S. size 2.5 (3 mm) needles, CO 22 sts and work back and forth in k2, p2 rib for 11 ¾ in (30 cm). BO and weave in ends on WS.

THE INSPIRATION FOR LOLITA came from the skulls and the magpies we bought from an old taxidermist in Paris. That's how she ended up as the punk girl in the book.

Chapter 11
Punk Lolita

We think Lolita might have misunderstood what it means to be a punk. She should be wearing all black, not wearing pink bows and such...

LOLITA

Outfit 18
A wide-striped sweater and black skirt with pink skulls and a pink edging. Lolita's hair is made with Royal Alpaca yarn and she has a matching pink bow.

1/2 Body

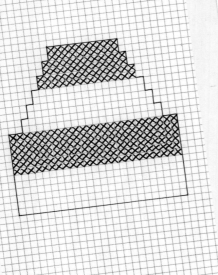

Whole Sleeve

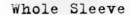
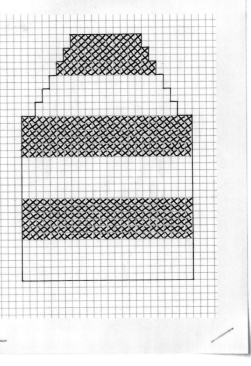

1/4 Skirt

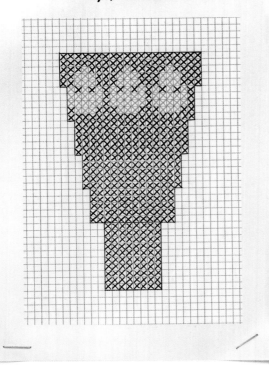

34. STRIPED SWEATER
BASIC PATTERN 3, PAGE 64
MATERIALS Dale of Norway Babyull:
Black 0090
Off white 0020

35. SKIRT WITH SKULLS
BASIC PATTERN 5, PAGE 67
MATERIALS Dale of Norway Falk:
Black 0090
Pink 4415

Knit the last round on the chart with needles U.S. size 1.5 (2.5 mm) and then bind off.
Crochet the edging: Work 1 sc in the last bound-off stitch, *ch 4, 1 sc in the 3rd edge st from the chain loop*; rep from * to * around. On the next round, work 5 sc in each chain loop; end with 1 sl st to first sc.
Weave in ends on WS and carefully steam press outfit.

OUTFIT 19

The black lace dress looks tough when worn over black pants. The scarf knitted with leftover yarns brightens up the outfit.

1/2 Body

36. LACE DRESS
BASIC PATTERN 12, PAGE 80
MATERIALS Dale of Norway Daletta:
Black 0090 (2 balls)

37 (33). STRIPED SCARF
BASIC PATTERN 20, PAGE 90

With U.S. size 2.5 (3 mm) needles, CO 22 sts and work back and forth in k2, p2 rib for 11 ¾ in (30 cm). BO and weave in ends on WS.

37. STRIPED ALPACA SWEATER (PAGE 137)
BASIC PATTERN 3, PAGE 64
MATERIALS Dale of Norway Royal Alpaca:
Red 4018
Black 0090

Work 4 rounds in each color, and then 10 rnds k2, p2 rib for the neck. We made the sweater with leftovers from the yarn basket.

Whole Sleeve

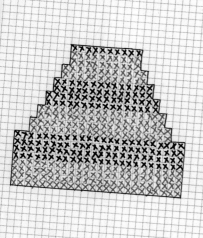

OUTFIT 20

The dress has 2 upholstery buttons
from an old sofa that match the
red stripes in the sweater.

1/4 Dress

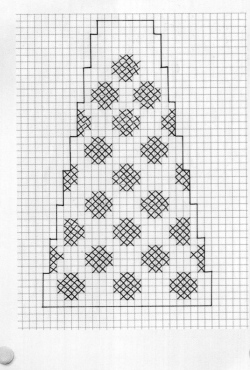

38. BLACK DRESS WITH WHITE POLKA DOTS
BASIC PATTERN 10, PAGE 76
MATERIALS Dale of Norway Falk:
Black 0090
Off white 0017

KNITTING IS
SO COOL!

1/2 Body

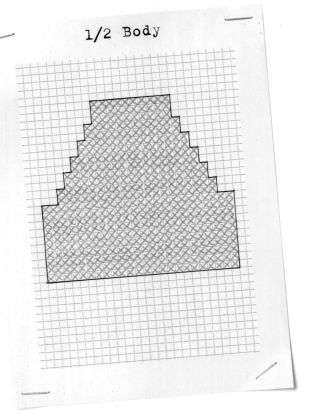

OUTFIT 21

The coat worn over the
thin striped sweater is
spiffed up with new
pirate buttons.

39. SHORT SLEEVE SWEATER
Basic Pattern 3, page 64
MATERIALS Dale of Norway Babyull:
Pale iris 5302
Pink 4504

Cast on with purple and work the
garter stitch edgings on the sleeves
and body as follows:
RND 1: Purl.
RND 2: Knit.
RND 3: Purl.
RND 4: Knit.
RND 5: Purl.
Continue, following the chart.
Finish the raglan shaping with 1
rnd purple before changing to nee-
dles U.S. 1.5 (2.5 mm). Use the same
color to work 30 rnds k2, p2 rib for
the neck.

40. LONG JACKET
Basic Pattern 14, page 84
MATERIALS Dale of Norway Falk:
Black 0090

Knit body until is 6 ¾ in (17 cm)
long to the armhole shaping.

Whole Sleeve

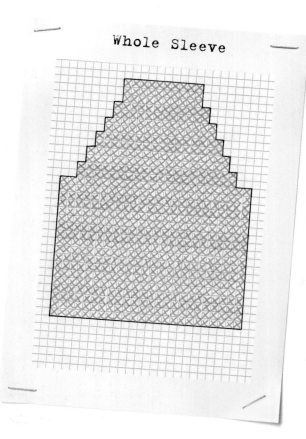

SHOW ME your record collection and I'll tell you who you are.

1/4 Skirt, Including Ribbed Edge

THE BEE MOTIF comes from *Norwegian Knitting Patterns* by Annichen Sibbern Bøhn.

THE INSECT SKIRT MAKES LOLITA RATHER SINISTER!

41. SWEATER WITH POCKETS
BASIC PATTERN 3, PAGE 64

The sweater was knit with leftover yarns from the yarn basket (ragg sock yarn) on needles U.S. 1.5 and 2.5 (2.5 and 3 mm).

Work the ribbing and then 20 rnds on the body. Pick up and knit 24 sts on the 1st round after the ribbing and work 20 rows back and forth in stockinette.
Row 21: Join pocket and body: K3 on needle 1, *knit 1 st from the pocket together with 1 st from the body*; rep from * to * and end with k3. Knit 2 rnds and then continue, shaping the armholes as in the basic instructions.

42. BEE SKIRT
BASIC PATTERN 5, PAGE 67
MATERIALS Dale of Norway Falk:
Grey heather 0007
Black 0090

OUTFIT 22

Here's a cool gray
sweater with pockets for
a tough girl. The insect
skirt makes her rather
sinister. But, with that bow
in her hair, well...

Outfit 23

When Lolita wants to dress up she usually wears this pink dress. We've adjusted the stitch count to make the dress a bit more ruffled. The black poncho with the skull embroidered on it is Lolita's favorite garment.

43. PONCHO WITH EMBROIDERED SKULL
BASIC PATTERN 16, PAGE 87
MATERIALS Dale of Norway Falk:
Black 0090
Silver yarn Lamé Metallic

The skull is embroidered on the skirt with duplicate stitch. See page 26 for more on how to embroider duplicate stitch. Keep the lower edge of the poncho smooth by crocheting edging as for the basic poncho.

44. PINK DRESS WITH CROCHETED BLACK EDGING
BASIC PATTERN 10, PAGE 76
MATERIALS Dale of Norway Daletta:
Fuchsia 4516
Black 0090

X on the chart = drop the stitch down

The dress features a black crocheted edging and pink buttons from the sewing box. At each X on the chart, drop 1 stitch. Do not work k2tog when shaping near an X.

75. MITTENS
BASIC PATTERN 21, PAGE 90
MATERIALS Dale of Norway Falk:
Fuchsia 4516

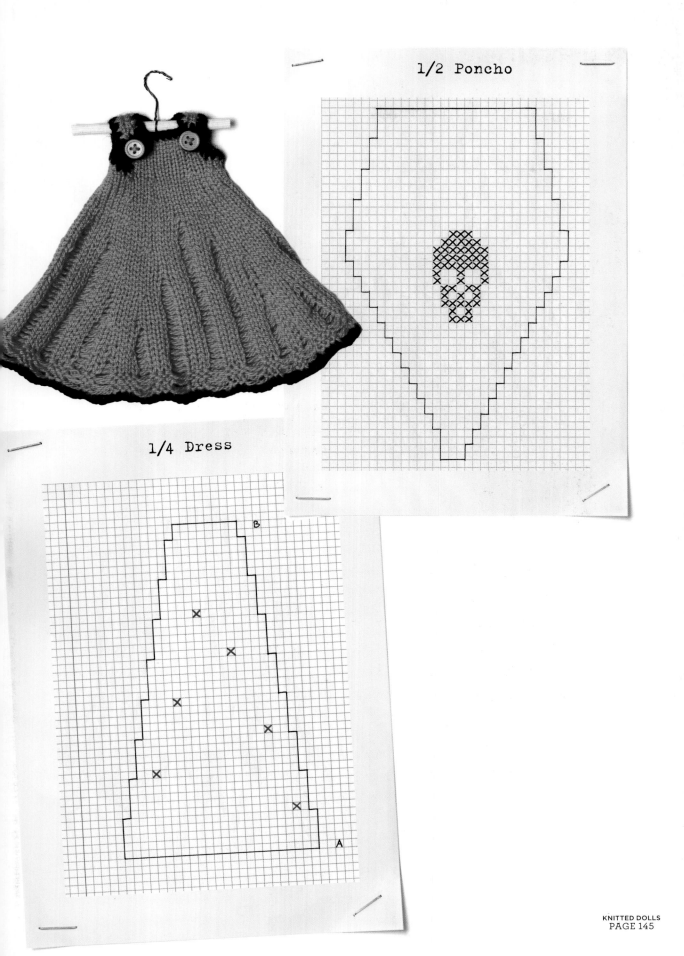

1/2 Poncho

1/4 Dress

*I saw a ship sailing on the
sea's watery way,
and the ship was filled with
good things for you.*

From *Rhymes and Rules for Every Child*, retold in
Norwegian by Alf Prøysen.

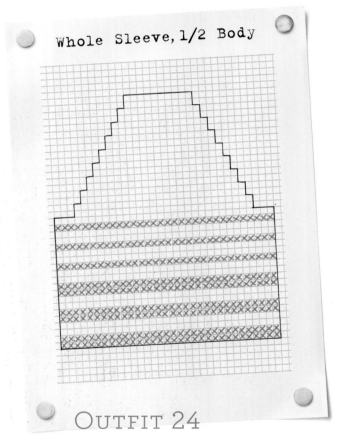

Whole Sleeve, 1/2 Body

OUTFIT 24

Set sail in this blue and white
striped sweater. This sweater
was inspired by the woman at
the fore of a large sailboat in our
scrapbook.

45. MARITIME SWEATER
BASIC PATTERN 2, PAGE 60
MATERIALS Dale of Norway Falk:
Indigo blue 5764
Natural 0020

Cast on with blue and work 5
rnds in k2, p2 rib for the edges
of the sleeves and body. The
neck finishes with 10 rnds k2,
p2 rib.

46. BLUE SHORTS
BASIC PATTERN 7A, PAGE 69
MATERIALS Dale of Norway Falk:
Indigo blue 5764

OUTFIT 25

Milton's surfer outfit. Did you notice how just a little bit of the bathing suit shows—that's the trend these days. Salt water and a humid climate are great for curly hair.

Milton

1/2 Shorts, Including Ribbed Edge

47. SPOTTED SHORTS
BASIC PATTERN 7A, PAGE 69

These shorts are not as long as the other shorts as they are knit with two colors and are a little thicker. The chart includes the garter stitch and ribbed edgings.

MATERIALS
Yarn suitable for needles U.S. 1.5 and 2.5 (2.5 and 3 mm), for example, Dale of Norway Falk:
Deep blue 5545
Natural 0020

OUTFIT 26

An embroidered heart on the sweater sleeve is as tough-looking as a tattoo but it hurts less. This sweater is Milton's favorite, knit for him to wear as autumn approaches.

1/2 Body

Whole Right Sleeve

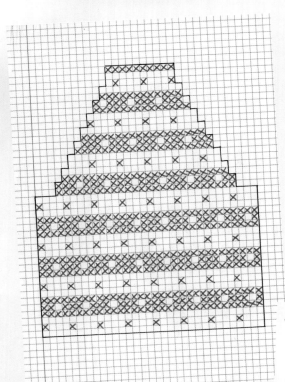

Whole Left Sleeve

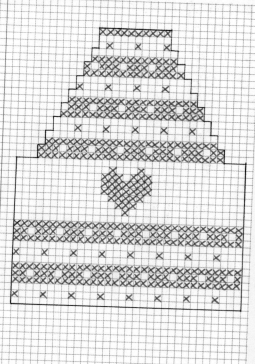

48. BOYFRIEND SWEATER
BASIC PATTERN 2, PAGE 60
MATERIALS Dale of Norway Falk:
Electric blue 5646
Natural 0020
Burgundy 4227

Embroider the heart on the sleeve with
duplicate stitch (see page 26).

49. GREEN SHORTS
BASIC PATTERN 7A, PAGE 69
MATERIALS Dale of Norway Falk:
Lime green 8817

OUTFIT 27

Milla's dress sports a sea motif adapted from a sailor's sweater in one of our collections. That was inspired by the 1948 *Women and Clothing Knitting Book*. The pattern was a bit oversized for the little doll so it now resembles a type of sea urchin.

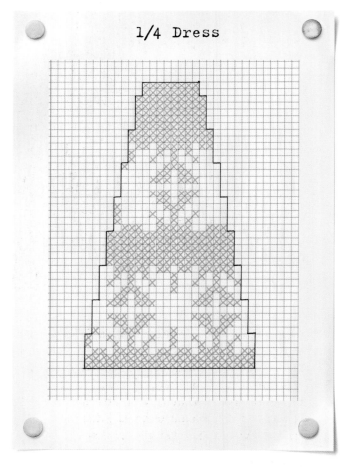

1/4 Dress

50. DRESS WITH SEA MOTIF
BASIC PATTERN 10, PAGE 76
MATERIALS Dale of Norway Falk:
Deep blue 5545
Putty 2425

Outfit 28

The jacket is edged with waves inspired by
the Greek border pattern "running dog." The
buttons are old. The shoes are seamed with
back stitch to make them sporty
sailor's shoes. See Chapter 3 (p. 25) for
how to embroider back stitch.

Whole Sleeve, 1/2 Body

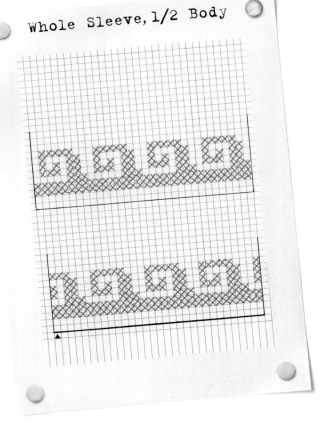

51. JACKET WITH WAVE PATTERN

Basic Pattern 14, page 84
The chart for the body shows half of the
border and the arrow indicates the center
back.

MATERIALS Dale of Norway Daletta:
Midnight blue 5473
Natural 0020

Cast on with U.S. size 1.5 (2.5 mm)
needles and blue. Work 1 rnd k2, p2 rib
with blue; change to white and work 2
rnds rib. Finish the ribbed edging with
2 rnds blue. Work the same striped rib
edge on the sleeves. At the neck, begin
the ribbing with 2 rnds blue, then 2 rnds
white and 1 rnd blue. BO with blue. Single
crochet along the right side of the front,
making chain loop buttonholes. Edge the
left front with a row of single crochet.

11. RED PANTS

Basic Pattern 7A, page 69
MATERIALS Dale of Norway Falk:
Burgundy 4227

OUT IN THE GARDEN

The garden at Tonsåsen where we live has been a huge source of inspiration for us. In it we often find the most unbelievable color combinations imaginable. During a trip to England in 2010, we learned the English expression "garden people" lovely and eccentric personalities that we can really relate to. After that we had to make some outfits that the dolls could wear out in the garden.

KRYSTEL

KRYSTEL'S HAIR is held up by pipe cleaners decorated with new buttons. Work gloves in Falk Red 4137. The shoes are decorated with large, vintage buttons.

OUTFIT 29
Use leftover yarns to embroider as many flowers as you like on this dress.

52. SWEATER WITH HEART BUTTONS
BASIC PATTERN 14, PAGE 84
MATERIALS Dale of Norway Falk:
Dark olive 8972
The body is 3 ¼ in (8 cm) before the raglan shaping and the sleeves 2 ½ in (6.5 cm) before the raglan shaping.

53. DRESS WITH FLOWER EMBROIDERY
BASIC PATTERN 10, PAGE 76
MATERIALS Dale of Norway Falk:
Lavender 5224
Use remnants for the flower embroidery.

54. FLOWER SWEATER
Basic Pattern 13, page 82
MATERIALS Dale of Norway Falk:
Light sheep heather 2931
Dark turquoise 6215
Dandelion 2417

28. OVERALLS
Basic Pattern 7B, page 71
See also Outfit 15 in the chapter on candies, p. 126.

MATERIALS Dale of Norway Falk:
Soft blue 5943
Peony 4516

Outfit 30
We were really lucky to find old
buttons that perfectly matched
the flowers. Sew on the buttons
with yellow thread to match
the flower centers.

BEHIND THE SCENES: We set up the garden scene on
an old shop counter that we have on the veranda.

WE'RE TAKING a well-earned break between chores.

SISSEL ❀ KRYSTE

Outfit 31

When she ties her scarf on this way, Agnethe might remind you of Grace Kelly. The basic pants are transformed into jogging pants with ribbing at the edges of the legs.

55. LONG SWEATER
BASIC PATTERN 14, PAGE 84
MATERIALS Dale of Norway Falk:
Cyclamen 4536
Make the sweater body 4 ¼ in (11 cm) long before the armhole shaping.

56. JOGGING PANTS
BASIC PATTERN 7A, PAGE 69
MATERIALS Dale of Norway Falk:
Pink 4415
Begin the legs by working 5 rnds k2, p2 rib on needles U.S. 1.5 (2.5 mm).

33. STRIPED SCARF
BASIC PATTERN 20, PAGE 90
MATERIALS Dale of Norway Falk:
*Work 4 rows Purple 5226, 4 rows Pink 4401 and repeat from * until scarf is about 11 ¾ in (30 cm) long. With U.S. size 2.5 (3 mm) needles, CO 22 sts and work back and forth in k2, p2 rib for 11 ¾ in (30 cm). BO and weave in ends on WS.

Agnethe

OUTFIT 32

The shoes are embellished with new buttons.
Her hair pin is a flower cut out of
an old ribbon.

1/4 Skirt, 1/2 Top

SIV

57. SUNFLOWER DRESS
BASIC PATTERN 11, PAGE 78
MATERIALS Dale of Norway Falk:
Dandelion 2417
Orange 3309

Our insect collection helped us choose the colors for this outfit. Many years ago we visited a shop in Paris that sold dried insects and butterflies. We go back to the shop every time we are in Paris and always bring home more insects. The insects are so diverse and have so many beautiful colors that we use them as inspiration for color combinations and styles.

OUTFIT 33

58. RED SWEATER
BASIC PATTERN 13, PAGE 82
MATERIALS Dale of Norway Falk:
Poppy 3609

59. DRESS WITH BUTTERFLY MOTIFS
BASIC PATTERN 10, PAGE 76
MATERIALS Dale of Norway Falk:
Cocoa 3072
Natural 0020
Poppy 3609 for duplicate stitch embroidery

WORK SINGLE CROCHET around the neck opening of the dress, adding a chain loop at the end of each strap for the button loop. Make the chain loop as long as necessary to go around the button. On this model, there are 3 sc at the end of the loop, ch 4, 1 sc in the first corner, and 5 sc in the chain loop back. Work 2 sc in the corners where the crochet swings inwards.

FOR INSTRUCTIONS on decorating the wings and antennae on the butterflies with duplicate stitch, see Chapter 3, page 26.

1/4 Dress

Outfit 34

The colors in this sweater are the same as on an insect in our collection with striped legs. The bee stripes are made with duplicate stitch in yellow and the skirt is edged with single crochet.

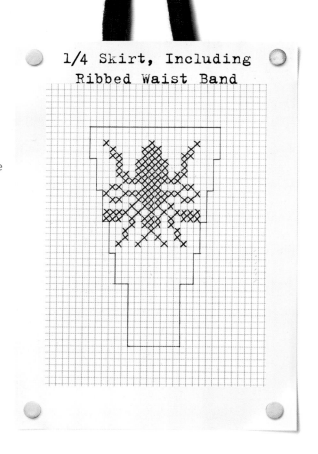

Krystel

60. SWEATER WITH MULTICOLOR STRIPES
BASIC PATTERN 3, PAGE 64
MATERIALS Dale of Norway Falk:
Lime green 8817
Dandelion 2427
Barn red 4137
Pink 4415

61. SKIRT WITH BEES
BASIC PATTERN 5, PAGE 67
MATERIALS Dale of Norway Falk:
Barn red 4137
Black 0090
Dandelion 2427 for duplicate stitch embroidery

After binding off, work 1 round sc on the lower edge of the skirt, with 1 sc in each bound-off stitch.

For instructions on duplicate stitch embroidery for the bees' yellow stripes, see Chapter 3, page 26.

1/4 Skirt, Including Ribbed Waist Band

1/2 Body, Including Ribbed Edge

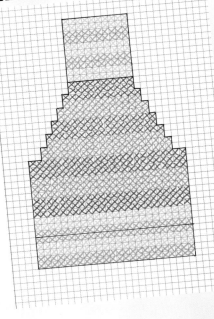

Whole Sleeve, Including Ribbed Edge

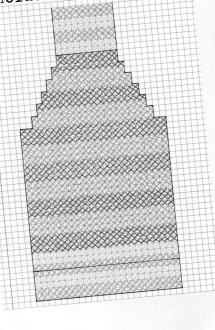

ONE OF THE BUTTERFLIES from Paris has landed on Sissel's arm.

OUTFIT 35

Here's yet another variation of
a sweater with multicolor
stripes. Also part of the insect
and butterfly collection.

62. STRIPED SWEATER
BASIC PATTERN 3, PAGE 64
MATERIALS Dale of Norway Falk:
Lime green 8817
Norwegian blue 5744
Dandelion 2427
Poppy 3609

6. GREEN PANTS
BASIC PATTERN 7A, PAGE 69
MATERIALS Dale of Norway Falk:
Fern green 9155

The legs on these pants are 5 ¼ in (13 cm) before binding off.

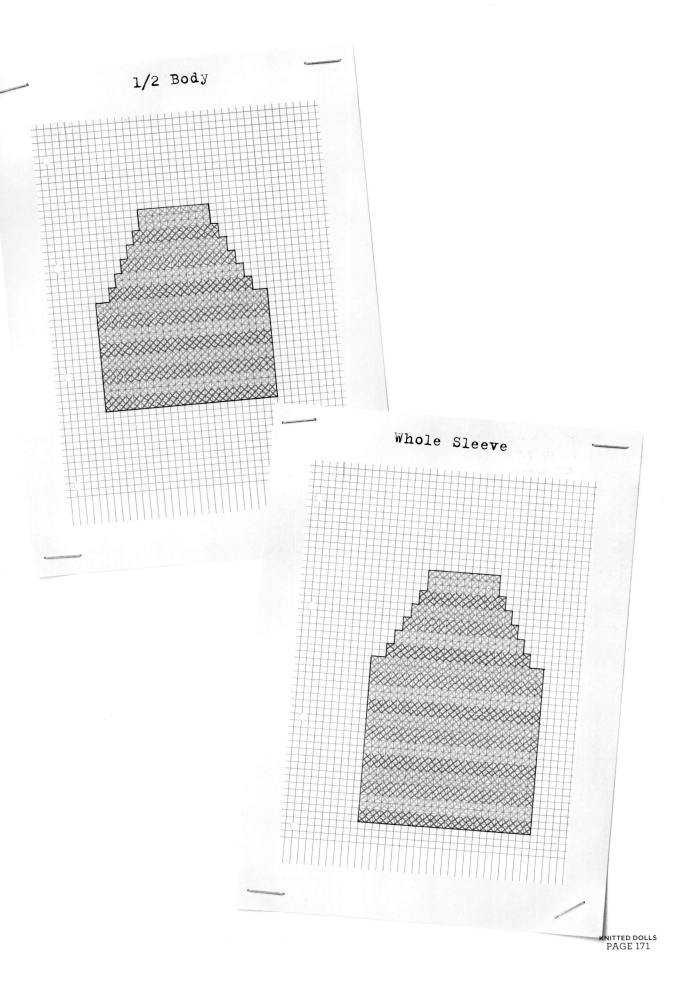

1/2 Body

Whole Sleeve

CHAPTER 15

HEN KNITTING

We used to knit a lot of sweaters with small patterns worked with leftover yarns. We called these "hen knitting." It must have been over 20 years ago, when we sat around the fire with our guitars and knitted mostly with purple and green yarns.

While we're on the theme of hen knitting: We have chickens but while they are producing eggs they stay at the house of a nephew in Gausdal. As long as they lay eggs, they'll stay there but afterwards, they can come home to us—to our old age home for hens which have finished laying.

This section features garments in many colors. We have taken our inspiration from some wooden birds we found in Oaxaca, Mexico.

OUTFIT 36

This sweater features pattern borders inspired by motifs and colors on some handpainted Mexican wooden birds. There are a lot of ends so we cut the yarns rather than carrying them up and wove in the ends when finishing.

Ulla

Whole Sleeve, 1/2 Body

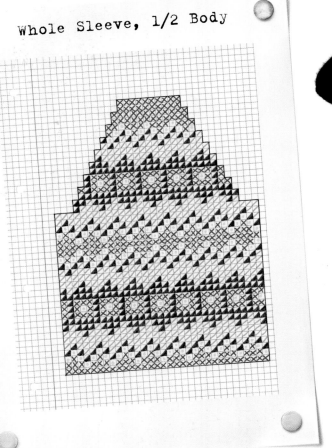

63. LONG SWEATER IN HEN KNITTING
BASIC PATTERN 2, PAGE 60
MATERIALS Dale of Norway Babyull:
Red 3718
Brown 3871
Pastel pink 4711
Yellow lurex yarn / Fingering

1/4 Dress

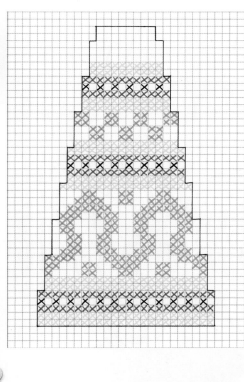

OUTFIT 37

64. SHORT SWEATER
BASIC PATTERN 13, PAGE 82
MATERIALS Dale of Norway Falk:
Aquamarine 6604
Dark turquoise 6215

Wind two little balls of dark turquoise and work the garter stitch lower edge from one ball. Work each button band with a separate ball of yarn; twist the light and dark yarns over each other when changing from the body to the band. Knit the garter stitch neck band with dark turquoise.

65. DRESS WITH BIRD MOTIF
BASIC PATTERN 10, PAGE 76
MATERIALS Dale of Norway Falk:
Putty 2425
Goldenrod 2427
Red 4018
Aquamarine 6604
Off white 0017
Black 0090

OUTFIT 38

This short sweater is easier to knit than the long sweater in the same style—there's less to keep track of. The simple red skirt is knit with the same red yarn as the sweater.

66. SHORT SWEATER IN HEN KNITTING
BASIC PATTERN 2, PAGE 60
MATERIALS Dale of Norway Falk:
Cocoa 3072
Blossom pink 4203
Red 4018
Yellow

67. RED SKIRT
BASIC PATTERN 5, PAGE 67
MATERIALS Dale of Norway Falk:
Red 4018

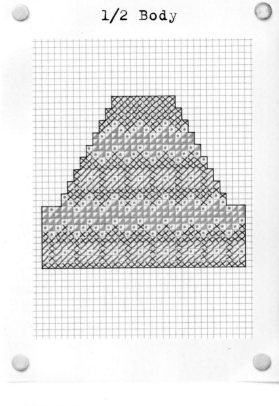

1/2 Body

Whole Sleeve

OUTFIT 39

Ulla has toned down the outfit with a simple purple sweater worn over a patterned skirt. The panel motifs are once again taken from our Mexican wooden birds.

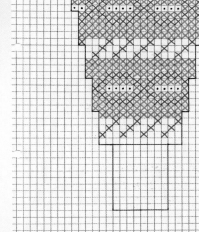

1/4 Skirt, Including
Ribbed Waist Band

68. THICK SWEATER
BASIC PATTERN 4, PAGE 66
MATERIALS Dale of Norway Freestyle:
Grape 5245

69. SKIRT IN HEN KNITTING
BASIC PATTERN 5, PAGE 67
MATERIALS Dale of Norway Babyull:
Mushroom 2621
Chambray 5914
Light green 9013
Navy 5755
Tangerine 2817
Yellow lurex yarn / Fingering

Outfit 40

70. TOP WITH BIRD MOTIFS
BASIC PATTERN 2, PAGE 60

This pattern comes from the remnant of
a bazaar prize – a blanket produced by
Th. Lunde in Lillehammer. The pattern
on the blanket is from an old spot weave
from Gudbrand Valley.

MATERIALS Dale of Norway Falk:
Pastel yellow 2313
Red 4018
Dark turquoise 6215
Iris purple 5144

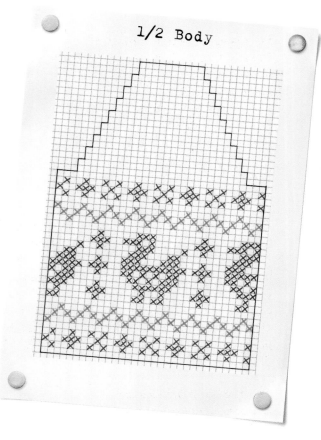

1/2 Body

Ulla

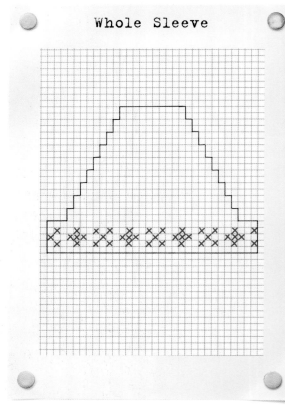

Whole Sleeve

71. JUMPSUIT IN HEN KNITTING
BASIC PATTERN 9, PAGE 73
MATERIALS Dale of Norway Falk:
Grey heather 0007
Red 4018
Dark turquoise 6215
Orange 3309
Pastel yellow 2313
Black 0090
Off white 0017

OUTFIT 41
This is the hardest garment in the series to make. To simplify it, the yoke is all grey heather. The buttons are vintage.

The leg repeats are worked two times. The sleeves have red ribbed edges and the pattern begins with 2 rounds of grey heather. For the placket with the button bands, the first stitch is knit when beginning with a new color; if the round begins with the same color as the previous round, slip the first stitch. Bind off for the armholes on the wrong side: P12, BO 6, p24 (including last stitch from bind-off), BO 6, p12 (including last stitch from bind-off).

Join the body and sleeves:
Continue raglan shaping for the sleeves and body until 30 stitches total remain. Work the last decreases only on the sleeves. Finish the body with 1 purl row in the same color as the ribbed neckband.

1/2 Jumpsuit

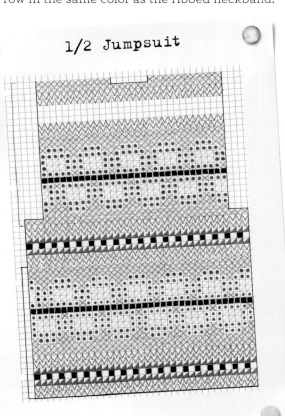

ULLA'S CROCHETED PILLOW

THE PILLOW IS CROCHETED *with DMC embroidery yarn. Use one strand of the yarn and hook U.S. size 9 (1.5 mm). Begin with ch 6 and join into a ring with 1 sl st into first ch. Ch 4 (= 1 tr), 3 tr, ch 3, (4 tr, ch 3) 3 times; end with 1 sl st into top of ch 4 at beginning of round. Change colors and, beginning at a corner, work the final round: (Ch 4, 3 tr, ch 3, 4 tr) in corner loop, ch 2, *(4 tr, ch 3, 4 tr) in next corner, ch 2*; rep from * to * two more times and end with 1 sl st into top of ch 4 at beginning of rnd. Cut yarn and weave in all tails on WS.*

THE FINISHED PILLOW *consisted of 12 blocks sewn together with regular sewing thread. Make a cotton pillow case and fill it with washed wool. Sew the crocheted cover onto the front of the pillow, stitching in each chain loop and with one stitch between each of the blocks.*

CHAPTER 16
PAJAMA PARTY

*It was a lovely, lovely day, but now it's over,
and everyone, all of them really nice, has lain down to sleep.
And the sky which was mild and blue with many thousands of smiles in it,
begins first to laugh again early in the morning.*

*Evening song about spring—Thoralf Borg from
Song Book for the Schools by Mads Berg*

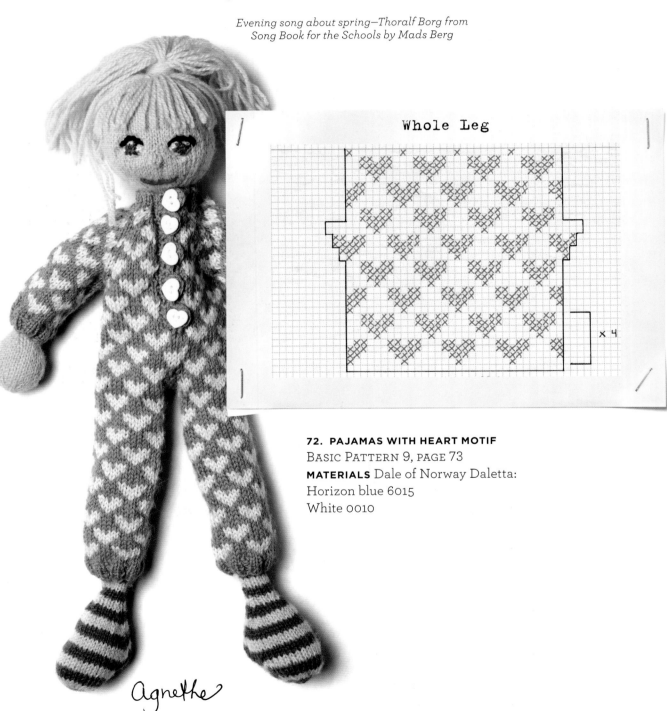

72. PAJAMAS WITH HEART MOTIF
BASIC PATTERN 9, PAGE 73
MATERIALS Dale of Norway Daletta:
Horizon blue 6015
White 0010

1/2 Body, Left Side

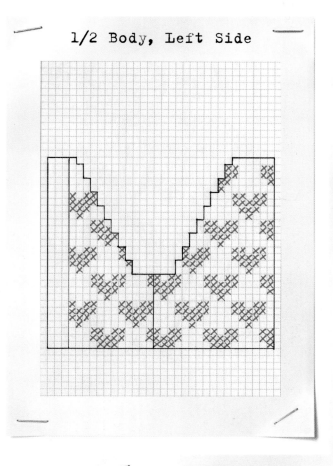

1/2 Body, Right Side

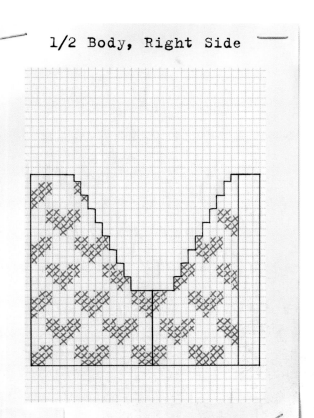

Whole Sleeve

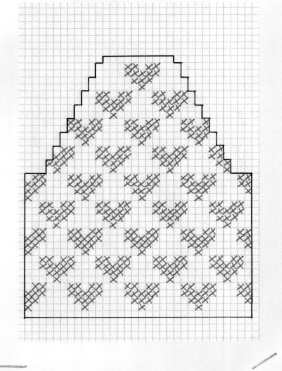

OUTFIT 42

A comfy pattern for
the pajamas with
new heart buttons.

OUTFIT 43

A solid color jumpsuit needs
cute buttons for decoration.
This outfit has new buttons
with little cats.

SiV

73. YELLOW JUMPSUIT
BASIC PATTERN 9, PAGE 73
MATERIALS Dale of Norway Falk:
Yellow 2106

Outfit 44

A dress with a multipurpose design, in this case it's a night-gown. See also Outfit 19 in Chapter 11 on Punk Lolita.

Sissel 🌸

74. NIGHTGOWN
Basic Pattern 12, page 80
See also Outfit 19 in Goth-Lolita, Chapter 11
MATERIALS Dale of Norway Daletta:
Natural 0020 (2 balls)

Chapter 17
Conclusion

It has been a long day and we have had a lot of fun.

We are finished playing with the dolls for today, of course we can play with them in the morning or on another day. The dolls are spread out in every room of the house; on the floor, table-tops and shelves, yes, everywhere. What the dolls do when we leave the room and turn out the light, *we will perhaps never know...* One thing is certain—they won't go back in the cupboards. But, that's how it is. We hope you will have as much fun as we have. *Good night!*

A THOUSAND THANKS to everyone who has worked with us on this book! Thanks to Gina and Pål, our editor, Inger-Margrethe and everyone at Cappelen Damm. Thanks to the knitting ladies at Dale of Norway as well as Tomally Nerjordet for help with the knitting. And last, but not least, a big thanks to photographer Ragnar and stylist Inger for four unforgettable and fun days with lots of play and fun at Tonsåsen station.

SISSEL WAS LEFT OUT on the veranda. It's a good thing she is made of wool so it won't hurt if she gets a little damp during the night.

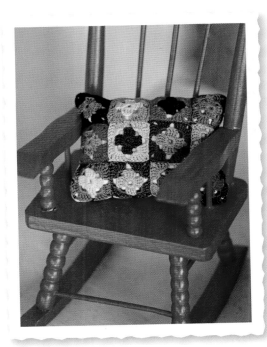

ULLA HAS LEFT THE ROCKING CHAIR. Where can she have gone?

NOW ALL WE HAVE TO DO is pick up the dolls and put them away until the next time someone visits.
Maja almost got all the way home and in her chest.

INSTRUCTIONS FOR THE KNITTED DOLLS ~~check~~ ~~with~~

MATERIALS

2 sets of 5 dpn U.S. size 1.5 (2.5 mm)
Yarn for the body and hair: FALK see page 17.
Wool stuffing 2.8 oz (80 g).

The doll must be knitted firmly, so use a smaller size needle if necessary. The wool stuffing shouldn't come out through the body or show through.

RIGHT LEG

With needles U.S. 1.5 (2.5 mm), CO 8 sts.
Divide sts evenly over 4 dpn = 2 sts on each needle.
Join, being careful not to twist cast-on sts.
RND 1: K8.
RND 2: *K1, inc 1, k1*; rep from * to * around.
RND 3: K12.
RND 4: *K1, inc 1, k1, inc 1, k1*; rep from * to * around.
RND 5: K20.
RND 6: *K1, inc 1, k3, inc 1, k1*; rep from * to * around.
Knit 8 rnds or ¾ in (2 cm). ~~2 knit then~~ 8
Weave in yarn end at tip of toe neatly on WS and then stuff foot with wool.

HEEL 2 knit then 8·stst

Over half of the stitches, work 8 rows stockinette (knit 1 row, turn and purl 1 row), beginning with a knit (RS) row.

Continue by working over all 4 needles as follows:
NDL 1: K7.
NDL 2: Pick up and knit 5 sts from the side of the heel with ndl 2 and k12.
NDL 3: K7.
NDL 4: Pick up and knit 5 sts from the other side of the heel with ndl 4 and k12.

LEGS AND THIGHS k19

RND 1: K7, k2tog, k27, ~~k2tog.~~

14 sts

RND 2: Knit around.
RND 3: K7, k2tog, k25, k2tog.
RND 4: Knit around.
RND 5: K7, k2tog, k23, k2tog (pink) (legs) (thighs)
RND 6: Knit around.
RND 7: K7, k2tog, k21, k2tog.
RND 8: Knit around.
RND 9: K7, k2tog, k19, k2tog.
RND 10: Knit around.
RND 11: *K1, k2tog, k1, k2tog, k1*; rep from * to * around.
RND 12: K20.
RND 13: *K1, k2tog, k2*; rep from * to * around.
RND 14: K16.
RND 15: *K1, k2tog, k1*; rep from * to * around.
12 sts now remain.

Start the leg by dividing these 12 sts over 3 ndls = 4 sts per ndl and use the 4th ndl to knit with. Knit 70 rnds or 6 ¾ in (17 cm). Use a thread marker to indicate the beginning of the round. Stuff the leg with wool as you work. Use a pencil or something similar to push the wool down. Don't fill the piece all the way to the top to avoid the wool getting caught into the knitting.

FINISH THE LEG

RND 1: K1, inc 1, k10, inc1, k1.
RND 2: K14.
RND 3: K1, inc 1, k12, inc 1, k1.
RND 4: K16.
RND 5: K1, inc1, k14, inc 1, k1.
RND 6: BO 2 sts, k14 (including the last st from the bind-off), BO the last 2 sts.
Divide the leg sts over 2 dpn = 7 sts on each needle.

LEFT LEG

CO 8 sts onto the other set of dpn and follow the instructions for the right leg.
Finish the leg as follows:
RND 1: K5, inc 1, k2, inc 1, k5.
RND 2: K14.
RND 3: K6, inc 1, k2, inc 1, k6.
RND 4: K16.
RND 5: K7, inc 1, k2, inc 1, k7.

RND 6: K7, BO 4, k7 (including the last st from bind-off).

Divide the leg sts over 2 dpn = 7 sts on each needle.
Join the legs and knit over all sts.
Work 7 rnds or ¾ in (2 cm).
Sew the groin seam together and fill the legs with wool.

BODY AND ARMS
With a T-shirt

Change to the T-shirt color and knit 20 rnds or 1 ¾ in (4.5 cm)

RND 21: BO 2 sts, k10 (including last st from bind-off), BO 4 sts, k10 (including last st from bind-off), BO the last 2 sts.
Place the 10 front sts on one needle and the 10 back sts on another needle.

Begin the Arms
CO 8 sts with arm color and U.S. 1.5 (2.5 mm) needles; divide the sts evenly over 4 dpn = 2 sts on each needle.
RND 1: K8.
RND 2: K1, inc 1, k1*; rep from * to * around.
RND 3: K12.
RND 4: *K1, inc 1, k1, inc 1, k1*; rep from * to * around.
RND 5: K20.
RND 6: *K1, inc 1, k3, inc 1, k1*; rep from * to * around.
Knit 9 rnds or ¾ in (2 cm).
Weave the yarn end from tip of hand neatly on WS.

RND 16: *K1, k2tog, k1, k2tog, k1*; rep from * to * around.
RND 17: K20.
RND 18: *K1, k2tog, k2*; rep from * to * around.
RND 19: K16.
RND 20: *K1, k2tog, k1*; rep from * to * around.
Divide remaining 12 sts over 3 dpn = 4 sts on each needle.

Continue by knitting 35 rnds or 3 ¼ in (8 cm) with skin color. Fill the arm with wool as you work. Change to T-shirt color and knit 5 rnds.
LAST RND: BO 2 sts, k8 (including the last st from bind-off), BO the last 2 sts.
Put the 8 sts onto 1 dpn.
Make the other arm the same way.

KNITTING THE BODY AND ARMS TOGETHER
Raglan Shaping:
Divide the sts over 4 dpn, with 8 sts for each arm and 10 sts for the front of the body and 10 sts for the back.
RND 1: K10 for back, k8 for one arm, k10 for front and k8 for the other arm.
RND 2: Back: K1, k2tog, k4, k2tog, k1; arm: k8; front: k1, k2tog, k4, k2tog, k1; arm: k8.
RND 3: K32.
RND 4: *K1, k2tog, k2, k2tog, k1*; rep from * to * around.
RND 5: K24.
RND 6 (WITH T-SHIRT COLOR): *K1, k2tog, k2tog, k1*; rep from * to * around.
Knit the last rnd in the T-shirt color.

Seam the armholes and weave in all ends on WS.
Fill with wool.

Neck and Head
RND 1: K16.
RND 2: *K1, k2tog, k1*; rep from * to * around.
RNDS 3-8: Knit.
RND 9: *K1, inc 1, k1, inc 1, k1*; rep from * to * around.
RND 10: K20.
RND 11: *K1, inc 1, k3, inc 1, k1*; rep from * to * around.
RND 12: K28.
RND 13: *K1, inc 1, k5, inc 1, k1*; rep from * to * around.
RND 14: K36.
RND 15: *K1, inc 1, k7, inc 1, k1*; rep from * to * around.
RND 16: K44.
RND 17: *K1, inc 1, k9, inc 1, k1*; rep from *

to * around.
RND 18: K52.
RND 19: *K1, inc 1, k11, inc 1, k1*; rep from
* to * around.
RND 20: K60.
RND 21: *K1, inc 1, k13, inc 1, k1*; rep from
* to * around.
RNDS 22-24: Knit.

NOSE
RND 25: Knit the nose as follows:

NDL 1: K17.
NDL 2: K17.
NDL 3: K8, inc 5 by working (k1, p1, k1, p1,
k1) into the 9th st.
Turn and purl the 5 sts.
Turn and k5.
Turn and p5.
Finish nose on RS by knitting the 5 sts on
right ndl, and then pass the 2nd st over
the 1st st; do the same with the 3rd, the
4th, and then the 5th st. Pull the sts to-
gether and end with k8.
NDL 4: K17.

RND 26: K68.

BEGIN THE HOLES FOR THE EYES
RND 27:
NDL 1: K17.
NDL 2: K17.
NDL 3: K2, BO 4, k5 (including the last
st from bind-off), BO 4 sts, k2 (including
last st from bind-off).
NDL 4: K17.

RND 28:
NDL 1: K17.
NDL 2: K17.
NDL 3: K2, CO 4, k5, CO 4, k2.
NDL 4: K17.

RNDS 29-34: Knit.
RND 35: *K1, k2tog, k11, k2tog, k1*; rep
from * to * around.
RND 36: K60.
RND 37: *K1, k2tog, k9, k2tog, k1*; rep
from * to * around.

RND 38: K52.

Now prepare the eyes before you continue knitting:

KNITTED EYES
With desired eye color and dpn U.S. 1.5
(2.5 mm), CO 8 sts.

RND 1: With white, k8 sts on 1 needle. Cut
eye color and work with white only.
RND 2: Divide the 8 sts over 4 dpn = 2 sts
on each ndl. Work *K1, inc 1, k1* on each
of the 4 needles.
RND 3: K12.
RND 4: *K1, inc 1, k1, inc 1, k1*; rep from *
to * around.
RND 5: K20.
BO. Make another eye the same way.
Weave in ends on WS and carefully
steam press the eyes.

FINISH HEAD
RND 39: *K1, k2tog, k7, k2tog, k1*; rep
from * to * around.
RND 40: K44.
RND 41: *K1, k2tog, k5, k2tog, k1*; rep
from * to * around.
RND 42: K36.
Check to make sure that the throat is
filled properly. If it is empty, fill it up well
so that the head won't hang down when
the doll is finished.

RND 43: *K1, k2tog, k3, k2tog, k1*; rep
from * to * around.
RND 44: K28.
RND 45: *K1, k2tog, k1, k2tog, k1*; rep
from * to * around.
RND 46: K20.
RND 47: *K1, k2tog, k2*; rep from * to *
around.
RND 48: K16.
RND 49: *K1, k2tog, k1*; rep from * to *
around.
Cut yarn and pull end through remaining
12 sts.

BASIC CHARTS

Basic chart for undergarments

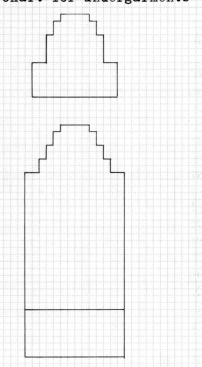

Basic chart for sweaters

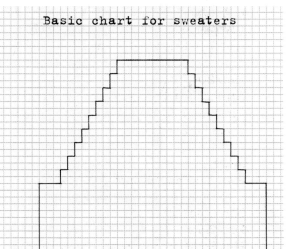

Basic chart for fitted sweaters

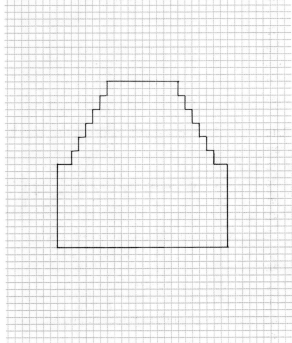

Basic chart for fitted sweater sleeves

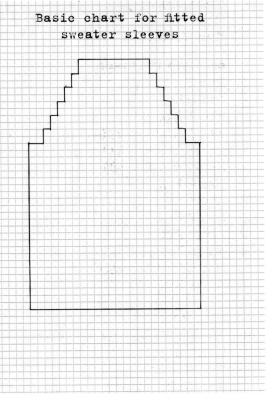

Basic Charts

Basic chart for thick sweaters

Basic chart for skirt

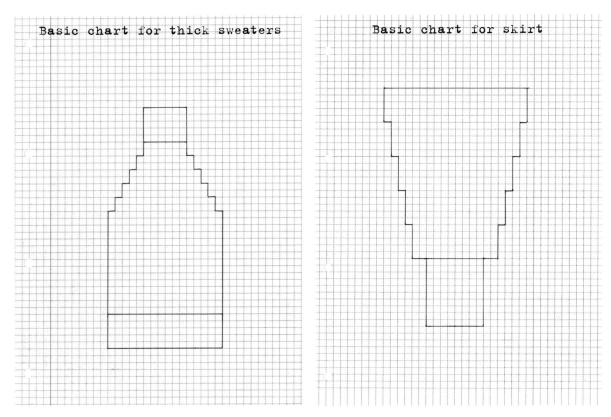

Basic chart for dress

Basic chart for dress with sleeves

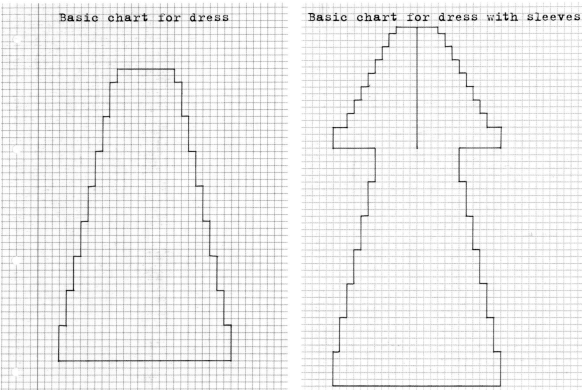

Basic Charts

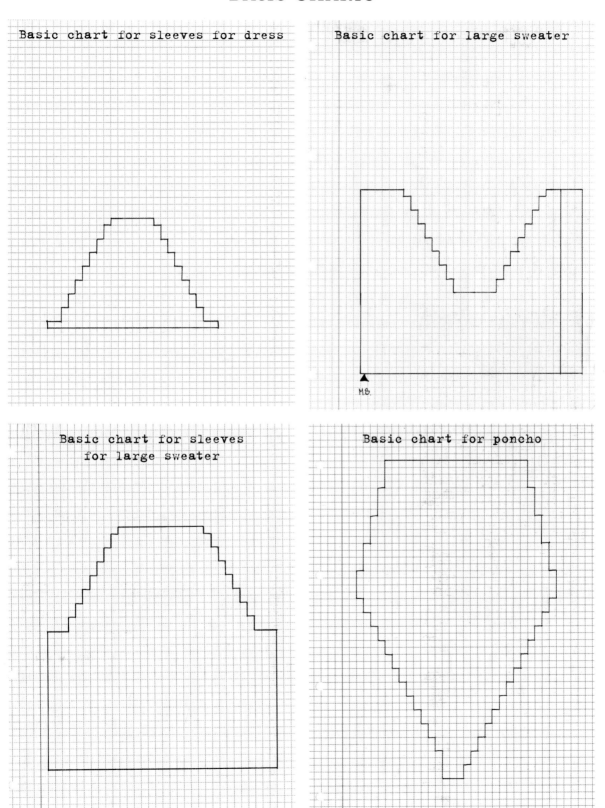

Basic chart for sleeves for dress

Basic chart for large sweater

MB.

Basic chart for sleeves
for large sweater

Basic chart for poncho

RESOURCES

The dolls were knitted with Dale of Norway 'Falk' (Sport/Light DK, 5-ply) yarn, and 'Falk', 'Heilo' (Sport/Light DK, 5-ply), 'Royal Alpaca' (Medium/Worsted, 10-ply) and 'Freestyle' (Medium/Worsted, 10-ply) for the clothes. Dale also sells wool top which you can use for stuffing the dolls. For more information see www.dalegarn.no.

Sandnes Garn's 'Peer Gynt' and 'Smart Superwash' are good substitutes for 'Falk'. Sandnes also makes wool tops. For more information about Sandnes, see www.sandnesgarn.no.

Rauma Garn's 'PT5' is Rauma's superwash wool which can also be used for the dolls. Rauma calls its wool stuffing 'Ullflor' (wool batting) which can be purchased in shops that sell Rauma and PT yarns. See www.raumaull.no.

The buttons we used in the book are from Hjelmtvedt. Visit www.hjelmtvedt.no for more information.

If you have difficulty in obtaining any of the yarns or materials mentioned in this book, suitable alternatives can be used instead.

Please visit our website www.arne-carlos.com or follow Arne & Carlos on Facebook for updates about us!

BIBLIOGRAPHY

Alle barns rim og regler [Every Child's Rhymes and Rules], retold in Norwegian by Alf Prøysen. Stabenfeldt Forlag. Stavanger, 1942.

Berg, Mads. *Skolens Sangbok* [Song Book for the Schools]. H. Aschehoug & Co. (W. Nygaard), Oslo, 1970.

Kamitsis, Lydia. Vionnet, Collection Mémoire de la Mode [Memory of Fashion Collection], Editions Assouline, Paris, 1996.

Kvinner og klærs strikkebok høsten 1948 [Women and Clothing Knitting Book, Fall 1948]. A/S Allers familie-journal.

Norsk institutt for bunad og folkedrakt Norwegian Institute for Costumes and Folk Clothing]. Fagernes. Sibbern Bøhn, Annichen. *Norwegian Knitting Designs*, reprint, Seattle, 2011.

Stickat nr. 3 [Knitting no 3]. Åhléns & Åkerlunds knitting division, 1946.